True Cost of Liberty
THE BURDEN OF FREEDOM

Forrest Haggerty

Title: True Cost of Liberty - The Burden of Freedom

by Forrest Haggerty © 2020

Cover by: Tim Lowry

Cover Photo of Rachel Lowry
used with permission by
Copyright owner: Tim Lowry
Edited by: Katie Lakina
Revised by: Tim Lowry

Published by: SpeakTruth Media Group, LLC.

Copyright © 2020 SpeakTruth Media Group, LLC. All Rights Reserved.

No part of this book may be reproduced, stored in a retrieval system, or transmitted without the written permission of SpeakTruth Media Group, LLC.

ISBN-13: 9781734264678

Table of Contents

Declaration of Independence 4
Preface 5
Introduction 11
Part I 15
Chapter 1 17
Chapter 2 29
Chapter 3 37
Chapter 4 49
Chapter 5 55
Chapter 6 67
Chapter 7 85
Chapter 8 93
Chapter 9 99
Chapter 10 115
Chapter 11 125
Chapter 12 135
Chapter 13 149
Chapter 14 157
Part II 165
Chapter 15 167
Chapter 16 179
Chapter 17 189
Chapter 18 207
Chapter 19 215
Chapter 20 229
Chapter 21 239
Conclusion 247
Dedication 251

Declaration of Independence

We hold these truths to be self-evident, that all men are created equal, that they are endowed by their Creator with certain unalienable Rights, that among these are Life, Liberty and the pursuit of Happiness.--That to secure these rights, Governments are instituted among Men, deriving their just powers from the consent of the governed, --That whenever any Form of Government becomes destructive of these ends, it is the Right of the People to alter or to abolish it, and to institute new Government, laying its foundation on such principles and organizing its powers in such form, as to them shall seem most likely to effect their Safety and Happiness.

— Congress, July 4, 1776

Preface

Gail was absent for one week after her son's death, and I could not stop thinking about her and what she must have been going through. When she returned, I did not know what to say to her. I did not know how to approach a person like her since I had never experienced it before. I wanted to say "I'm sorry," however, I could not help but think how fruitless those words would sound to a mother who had just lost her firstborn child in such a horrific manner. So, I did the only thing I could do at that time. I avoided her, and that always bothered me.

As the weeks and months passed, I would see her around campus and say "Hi" knowing she must have been suffering while the rest of us really had no clue what she was going through. I thought, 'What a burden she must carry,' and at that point the words, 'The Burden of Freedom' came to mind, and I began to see firsthand what a heavy load the cost of freedom carried. I realized that nearly every person who had made sacrifices in the United States military during a time of war carried 'The Burden of Freedom,' and those of us who have never been to war are completely removed from the reality of what our military personnel experience once they come home. Yet we are allowed to enjoy the benefits and freedoms they protected without truly knowing the burden that comes along with their sacrifices.

It was in January of 2004 when a colleague of mine told me that Gail Farnsworth's son, Jason Chappell, was killed by a car bomb in Iraq. My first reaction was shock, which was immediately followed by disbelief because these things always seemed to happen in some other city or some other far away state. Never before in my life had this type of tragedy hit so close to home. Jason was a local boy and his mother Gail worked in the front office of the school I taught at in Hemet, California.

Nearly a year and a half later, on June 14, 2006, another boy from Hemet, Michael Estrella, was killed. He was a Marine whose life was cut short in Iraq at the age of 20. One of his younger sisters became a student of mine the following school year. She wore a badge with his photo on it. When I asked her who was in the photo she told me then explained what happened to him. I remembered reading about it the previous June. Once again, I was stunned, and I felt deeply saddened for his family.

From January 24, 2004 to June 18, 2008 eleven individuals from the towns of Hemet and San Jacinto would give the ultimate sacrifice. Hemet and San Jacinto are so close together that a stranger passing through might have a hard time recognizing where Hemet ends and San Jacinto begins. Both towns are nestled in the San Jacinto Valley on the west side of the San Jacinto Mountains. Out of the eleven individuals who were killed, three were from San Jacinto and eight were from Hemet. A twelfth individual was from Aguanga, in the San Jacinto Mountains, twenty-two miles southeast of Hemet and a part of the Hemet Unified School District. For a short time, based on population percentage, the Hemet Unified School District had the highest death rate nationwide for the wars in Iraq and Afghanistan.

I never planned on writing a book about this subject, but as the boys from our valley kept falling, I felt compelled to at least attempt to share what I saw as a huge burden for our freedom. As a result, I looked closer into the meaning of freedom. Of course, I thought about our freedom of religion, freedom of speech, freedom of the press, freedom of association, and freedom of assembly; however, I was not completely satisfied with these as an absolute definition. These rights seemed more like necessary devices through which we express our freedom. Eventually, I came to see freedom as 'Individual Freewill,' which is a gift from all who have sacrificed in war. In American freedom, the uniqueness of the individual is valued and honored no matter what part of the world they come from. American freedom gives each of us the chance to reach our full potential, as well as the opportunity to find our reason, and fulfill our purpose for being on this earth. We are all given the opportunity to think freely and to be whoever God intended us to be under the umbrella of American freedom.

This can be a difficult concept to grasp for many Americans simply because they have nothing to compare it to. I remember growing up thinking that the rest of the world was just like America. Therefore, I had a hard time understanding the plight of other people in other countries. Many immigrants can fully grasp the concept because they come from those parts of the world where they are not valued and honored as individuals. Instead, they are controlled to the point where they are told what to think and how to think. If they fail to do what they are told they can face imprisonment and sometimes, death. The United States of America gives its citizens the freedom to be who they are born to be without hindrance and this freedom is protected by the military.

This book, "True Cost of Liberty: The Burden of Freedom," is my attempt to raise awareness about the reality of what our military personnel and their families endure so that the rest of us can remain free and safe from America's enemies. Unless we have experienced the price of freedom firsthand it is impossible to completely relate to it. It is my hope that the reader comes to a closer understanding of the reality of what all veterans of war and their families must deal with daily so the rest of the nation can enjoy the benefits of freedom.

Freedom is expensive, and those who reap its benefits are riding on the shoulders of those who bear its burden. Those who bear its burden are the family members who have lost a loved one and the military personnel who have sacrificed their mind, their body, and their spirit. They alone bear the burden of freedom, and we should not be so far removed from the reality of their experience that we become complacent or unaware of the heartache, physical pain, mental and emotional stress, and guilt they endure on a daily basis so the rest of us have the opportunity to peacefully be ourselves.

When I began writing this book I was not sure where it was headed. Unlike other books, it did not have a plan with a destination. Instead, it became the documentation of a journey based on other individuals' experiences. I would eventually figure out that I was simply along for a ride that took me to places in people's memories and emotions I never expected to go. The stories that were shared were primarily difficult confessions of traumatic experiences birthed from the unpleasant circumstances of war, which have challenged and forever changed the veterans and their families. Every day these individuals can struggle with one, some, or all of the psychological discomforts that post-war living has to offer. I underestimated the effect that these traumatic experiences had on those who bravely shared their experiences with me in this book. While some spoke freely and openly about their experiences in order to get something off their chest, others refused to say a word. Some began talking to me but would cut me off before my time with them was complete. It seemed to me they felt better off just not thinking about their experiences anymore. Emotional pain to the point of tears and anxiety were not uncommon among those who openly shared. I would also learn that guilt, sadness, melancholy and depression are very common for many of those who have served, and those who have lost a loved one. Therefore, in addition to trying to raise awareness, this book is also my way of saying, "Thank you for your sacrifices," and giving back to those who deserve all the benefits America has to offer. For without their dedication and sacrifices, we would not have the daily blessings we have. The fact of the matter is that a majority of troops who have been in battle are affected either physically, mentally, emotionally, or all of the above. Thousands of veterans have had to live with Post Traumatic Stress Disorder. Some have been able to conquer it while others continue to struggle and unfortunately, many have ended their own lives. Troops of various ages have had to make major adjustments in their lives in order to compensate for amputations or traumatic brain injury. Parents, grandparents, siblings, spouses, children, significant others, and friends all live in the emotional aftermath of an ultimate sacrifice, and witness the effects of Post Traumatic Stress Disorder. This is why I strongly feel this country owes its troops and the families of fallen heroes all it has to offer. They deserve money, houses, cars, free meals, and free education. After all these individuals have given, the least we could do is give them preferential treatment. It can never take away all their pain and suffering, but this display of gratitude can only help to lessen their anguish and assure them their sacrifices were not in vain.

Introduction

Most Americans are unaware that there are constant threats from countless enemies around the world who would love nothing more than to bring America to an end. Scrutinizing these enemies are agencies such as the National Security Agency (NSA), Central Intelligence Agency (CIA), and the Department of Defense (DoD). Unless we are directly employed by one of these agencies, we may be completely oblivious to the seriousness of these threats which hope to destroy our freedom, our culture, and our American way of life.

Everyday America faces a multi-array of enemy threats ranging from cyber-attacks on our internet infrastructure, to terrorist attacks from sleeper cells within our borders, to military strikes on our military resources and government facilities overseas. Through a joint effort between our government agencies, information is gathered, and if the evidence substantiates a genuine threat the President is immediately notified to decide on how best to confront it. These threats are continuous, and even the slightest pause can open a seam through which an enemy may implement a plot that could be disastrous to our country. Such was the case on September 11, 2001 when terrorists successfully used some of America's own resources to breach American shores and bring down the Twin Towers, plainly attacking America on its home turf and killing thousands of innocent civilians who were living well within what was thought to be a protected American mainland. It may be safe to say that at that time the victims of the Twin Towers, and nearly all Americans, were completely unaware of an enemy with such disdain and malicious intent focused on the downfall of America. However, threats toward America are not a new trend. America has dealt with attacks and the threat of attack since the Revolutionary War.

Since America's birth there have been over 300 known wars, skirmishes, evacuations, occupations, or interventions. There have also been numerous classified interventions by groups like SEAL Team-6 that are unknown to the American public. Essentially, America's fight for freedom may have officially ended in 1776, but it continues to be an ongoing saga because when one enemy is stopped another enemy appears.

America's modern-day enemies wear many masks, and as a result, varying degrees of threat require varying degrees of response. A cyber-attack, for example, is confronted in cyber space by members of the U.S. Cyber Command working for the National Security Agency (NSA). Biological warfare can be confronted with proper immunization. One of the more difficult possible threats to escape is a chemical attack because we normally do not walk around in protective clothing or carry a gas mask. Fortunately, biological and chemical agents tend to be more difficult for terrorists to acquire. Instead of biological and chemical agents, it would be much more plausible for a terrorist group to get their hands on a dirty bomb and the best line of defense against a dirty bomb is good intelligence. With proper intelligence, a terrorist threat can be met with a drone attack or Special Forces at its point of origin long before it is played out or long before it breaches American shores. Yet when a big enough threat turns to deed, America's military is usually called into action and America's military is not a single entity. It is a collection of hundreds of thousands of individuals who are specially trained in various fields of one of the five branches, and when working together they perform like a well-modified device capable of reaching anywhere around the world in order to protect human rights, our way of life, and our allies. However, in times of war the unfortunate reality of casualties is inevitable, and the military personnel on the front lines are the victims of these casualties.

According to the Department of Defense, at the end of WWII a total of 405,399 Americans had been killed. Of this group, 291,557 were classified as "Battle Deaths." In the Korean War there had been a total of 36,574 killed. Of this 33,739 have been categorized as "Battle Deaths." Vietnam massed a count of 58,220 deaths and 47,434 have been labeled as "Battle Deaths." The Persian Gulf War had 148 "Battle Deaths" with a total of 383 killed. The war in Iraq totaled 4,412 with 3,482 classified as "Hostile Deaths." In Afghanistan there was a total of 2,216 deaths and 1,833 have been listed as "Hostile Deaths." Any deaths categorized as "Battle Death" or "Hostile Death" is another way of saying these personnel were killed on the "Front Line," the point at which the battle takes place, the point at which an enemy either achieves their objective or is repelled. This is the threshold where America either perseveres or perishes.

If not for the efforts, hard work, and sacrifices of our military personnel, America could very well be a vulnerable and defenseless nation wide open to any enemy who wishes to breach our borders. Some may argue that America has been the aggressor in various conflicts, but history has shown that some aggression is necessary at times in order to ensure that an enemy does not methodically encroach on a nation over an extended period of time. This was the case in Korea and Vietnam. At the end of World War II, Communism began to expand into the Korean peninsula and French Indo China, which today is made up of Cambodia, Vietnam, and Laos. Under Communism citizens can be treated harshly and have no rights. They basically exist to serve their government of dictators. The United States of America knew that the uncontested spread of Communism could eventually reach around the world and take away the human rights of anybody living under its rules. As a result, America acted accordingly in Korea and Vietnam. Vietnam was not a popular war, but it was necessary in order to curb the potential for an all-out spread of Communism, and those protestors who have never had to live under the harsh laws of Communism are ignorant to the reasons why America is so resistant to it.

It is an unfortunate but absolute necessity for America to resist and fight her adversaries in order to perpetuate her existence. America's resistance to these foes is what guarantees our human rights, safety, and freedom. It would be ideal if no enemies existed and the earth was actually a peaceful place to live, but that is not reality at this point in history. The reality is such that America must continue to stand guard if future generations wish to reap the benefits of what the United States of America has to offer them, because history has proven that a country can have human rights and freedom stripped away without a military made up of millions of individual countrymen and women who are willing to sacrifice life, limb, and mind in order to uphold the security that protects the freedoms that America was founded on.

Part I
The Ultimate Sacrifice

*"Greater love has no one than this, than to
lay down one's life for his friends." John 15:13*

    The highest act of valor one has to offer his country is his life and many Americans have done exactly that since the Revolutionary War. All fallen troops are considered heroes, but when word of their sacrifice reaches home their community is rocked, and their family is devastated. Family members and friends are plunged into deep heartache by the person's abrupt departure. It is something that is not wished upon anybody, but it has happened to over a million Americans throughout America's history. As bystanders, we may recognize it is excruciating and may partially sense the pain, but we can never know it like family members and close friends do.

    With only memories the families and friends of fallen heroes struggle with the emotional trauma left behind from the loss of their loved one. Through photos, videos, recorded phone messages, emails, text messages, letters or belongings they remember what their dearly departed was once like, and can only imagine a future of what might have been. In an instant a family's hopes and dreams they envisioned for their loved one is stripped away and replaced with the burden of heartache. Unfortunately, as time heals, the heartache never completely ends.

Spc. Jason Kristoffer Chappell

Chapter 1
Spc. Jason Kristoffer Chappell

"Each of these heroes stands in the unbroken line of patriots who have dared to die that freedom might live and grow and increase in its blessings."

— *Franklin Delano Roosevelt*

". . . I could die anytime, any number of ways . . . but I'm here so you can remain free . . ."
— *Jason K. Chappell*

This was written in his last email sent to his mother.

Iraq
January 24, 2004

The explosives were methodically placed in the vehicle he would die in and nothing would impede his wish to indiscriminately ram into an American convoy to inflict random harm. Not even the thought of his own death would stop him. An average Iraqi, inconspicuous to Americans and very commonplace to his own people, who he was may never be known, but what he did is unforgettable to those in his aftermath. On the surface, he was just a common man in a run-of-the-mill car driving in an unassuming manner on an ordinary day in an ordinary place, the perfect way to mask the undercurrent of bad intentions housed in his basin of brutal thoughts. Knowing the exact time of the American shift change he waited patiently then drove through like countless peaceful Iraqis before him, only this time malevolence was the motive. This Iraqi would make a left turn and accelerate into the Humvee driver's door and detonate.

The concussive gust erratically blasted dirt, fragments, and debris hundreds of feet in various directions at supersonic speed. Nothing from the taxi or the suicide bomber could be found. Not even a tiny piece. The complete disintegration of his body and the car's existence was a testament to the force of the blast. However, the Humvee was not disintegrated. It lay in a field nearly fifty feet away upside down with no wheels, but still resembling a Humvee.

In July 2001, a confident 19-year-old Jason returned home one day and told his mother that he had just joined the Army and would soon be heading off to become a Ranger. Two hours prior he informed her that he was going to talk to the local recruiter. Not wanting him to join that day, Gail made sure to say, ". . . just ask questions, and do not join." She was hoping he would begin his college career after his graduation in June of 2000, but Jason wanted a break from academics after being a member of the Academic Decathlon Team at Hemet High School. He won thirteen medals while on the team his senior year. He was a straight A student, and he just wanted to do something different for a while, so he created a plan in his head to go to college using the GI Bill after completing his military service.

Being pre-September 11th and no looming threat of war on the horizon, Jason lacked any serious concerns. Perhaps he thought, 'Why not do something different and have it pay my college when I'm done?' A good break from a drab routine always does a person well. A change of pace that can turn a boy into a man.

Jason completed his basic training at Ft. Benning, Georgia in December 2001. The tall lanky 19- year- old was now a soldier. Originally his goal was to become a Ranger. However, after witnessing numerous injuries coming out of that program he chose a different path. He would move on to Ft. Hood, Texas and become part of Company B, 1st Battalion, 9th Cavalry to be converted into a Humvee driver.

Unlike California and the comforts of home Texas was a new experience for him. With the absence of nearby family members Jason spent a great deal of time online in chat rooms when he was not on duty. It was July 2, 2002 in a Yahoo chat room when Jason posted the message, *"Anyone on Fort Hood?"* His question was answered facetiously with, *"'On' Fort Hood? Don't you mean 'In' Fort Hood?"* It was Stephanie Davis. Her employer was in the middle of a move that day, and there was nothing for her to do so she sat at work and went into a chat room. The two chatted for the next eight hours and ended their day by exchanging numbers in order to continue with their correspondence. They chatted for several more hours on the phone afterwards.

The next day a fascinated, perhaps in love, Jason would not stop talking about Stephanie. He asked Sgt. Robert Stevenson to drive him to Fort Worth to meet her and a deal was struck. Sgt. Stevenson and his wife Kim were in the middle of a move and needed help. An energetic Jason helped them in exchange for a drive to Fort Worth, and on July 4th Sgt. Stevenson and Kim drove Jason to meet Stephanie. On the way there, Jason would not stop talking about Stephanie and on the way back he talked about her so much that Sgt. Stevenson and his wife were never given the chance to tell Jason how their own weekend went.

It was on Monday, August 5th, one month after the two met when they made it official. A laughing Stephanie said,

> "He rolled over from waking up that morning and I said, 'What are we going to do today?' He said, 'I think we should get married.' We discussed all the benefits of why we should get married and we agreed. Later in the day we went to the Tarrant County Court House and met my mom there on her lunch hour. She was the only witness and she paid for the marriage license. My mother is incredibly protective of me, which shows what a great guy Jason was. She would never have let me marry him had he not been a great guy. The only thing my mother said to Jason was, 'You might be getting a bad cook. You know she has never cooked for anybody. Are you sure you want to do this?'"

Within a few days the newlyweds were in California visiting Jason's family. At the conclusion of the first day Jason said, "Well mom, where are we going to sleep?" Gail said, "You're going to sleep in different rooms." Jason said, "But what if we are already married?" An unconventional approach to breaking the news to one's parents, but nonetheless, just as effective.

The implication that Gail was shocked would be an inescapable conclusion. For the longest of moments, she was beside herself. Gail would later say, "I love Stephanie dearly, but I would have loved to have met her before they were married."

Her first-born was married now. Her baby boy who was always smiling and had a habit of laughing in his sleep as a child. When his father would ask him why he was laughing he would say, "It's because the angels were tickling me."

Jason was born January 1, 1982. He was the firstborn child to Calvin David Chappell and Gail Lynn Chappell. He was also the first child of the new year born at San Dimas Community Hospital in San Dimas, California. Within hours of his birth he was diagnosed with respiratory distress and congenital heart disease. Doctors wanted to perform a heart catheterization with the possibility of open-heart surgery when he was two days old. Jason remained at the hospital for close observation prior to his scheduled surgery, but on the day of the surgery the doctor said to his parents, "We don't have to do the procedure. I can't really explain it but at 10:00 p.m. last night your son started showing improvement." His enlarged heart began returning to a normal size and the fluid in his lungs began clearing out. After six days he was sent home. On a follow up visit at ten days old the heart specialist said there were no signs of any problems. Jason was given a clean bill of health and the file was closed. From that day forward his parents referred to him as, "our miracle baby."

Like many children growing up, innocent mischief was a part of Jason's childhood. One night while brushing his teeth he decided to find out if a toothpaste tube could fly. He placed it at the edge of the porcelain sink with a portion of it hanging over the edge and instead of hitting it with his hand he hit it with a hammer that was left in the bathroom from some minor repairs that were being done. Needless to say, the porcelain sink was destroyed and the minor repairs had one major repair added to them. But a curious Jason did not stop there. On another occasion, Jason placed his mother's Tupperware plates and bowls in the oven then turned it on. When his parents came home they were at a loss for words after finding completely melted plastic in their oven.

When they asked him why he did it a young Jason answered, "I wanted to see what would happen to them."

When Jason was eight years old his sister Lisa Renae Farnsworth was born to Gail and Mitchell Farnsworth. There was now a total of four family members. However, as Jason grew older he decided to go live with his biological father David for the remainder of his elementary school years. Eventually, Jason would be back at his mother's home to attend middle school in Perris, California. At the conclusion of his middle school years his family moved to Hemet, California where Jason began his freshman year at Hemet High School

Stephanie and Jason were able to enjoy their holy bond of matrimony for one year in Texas before Jason was deployed to Iraq in September 2003 as a Humvee driver for Company B, 1st Squadron, 9th Calvary. For nearly six months he participated as a member of the massive team doing the groundwork for Operation New Dawn in Iraq.

Meanwhile Stephanie created new bonds with the wives whose husbands were at war, and she found morale and emotional support from this unassuming group of devoted women. Stephanie said, "They became a second family to me." These are women whose sacrifices measure up equally to their husband's sacrifices, but they are rarely recognized for it. They are the silent partner and just as important as their hero. They are the ones who wait patiently, faithfully, and loyally, some with children, some without, and all with the hope of never receiving that dreaded news that lies in the back of their minds. They know it is a possibility, but truly believe it will actually happen to someone else.

Jason's wife Stephanie was visiting her parents in Fort Worth, Texas that Sunday. She said,

"My friend Lauri drove me to my parents and while I was there Fox News had this big deal on T.V. about 12 soldiers being killed in explosions west of Falluja, and they mentioned that a Humvee driver was killed. I was concerned because Jason was a Humvee driver and I knew he was west of Falluja. I immediately called his unit and spoke to a young kid. When I told him who I was he kept saying, 'Everything is going to be okay, everything is going to be okay, let me give you my wife's number.' I didn't even know this kid. I knew something was seriously wrong at this point so I had Lauri drive me back to Fort Hood. That was the longest two-and-a-half-hour drive ever."

Stephanie's cell phone battery ran out in Fort Worth, and she left her charger in Fort Hood at Lauri's house. Upon arriving back at Lauri's house, she plugged her phone in and saw she had several messages. She was in the process of moving from her civilian apartment to on-base housing, and both her civilian neighbors and her military neighbors were telling her that the Army was looking for her. When her phone had enough battery, she called her friend Kim Stevenson, the wife of Sergeant Robert Stevenson. Kim agreed to meet up at Stephanie's home on base.

Five minutes later Stephanie arrived. She and Kim sat on the couch. Stephanie said,

"I was already crying and tried to stop to have a normal conversation but about thirty seconds after we sat on the couch three guys in uniform walked in and asked me if I was Stephanie Chappell, the wife of Jason Chappell. When I said yes, they said, 'We regret to inform you that your husband Jason has been killed in the line of duty.' I remember I fell to the floor crying and I kept saying, 'What do I do now? What do I do now? The Chaplin hugged me and stayed with me for a couple of hours until my family got to my house. After my family arrived the casualty assistance officer had to come by. They have paperwork you immediately have to sign. They also know you are going to need financial assistance so they gave me a check the day Jason died and that was the worst feeling in the world.

Looking back, I wished I would have called Jason's mother and told her myself, but I was only 22 years old and I didn't know what to do so when they asked me if I wanted the Army to inform his mother I said yes."

On the same day, a government vehicle pulled up to the Farnsworth's home in Hemet, California at about 3:00 p.m. Gail said,

"We were going into Farmer Boys to have breakfast that morning and Mitchell noticed in the newspaper stand a headline that said five more soldiers were killed in Iraq and he never reads the headlines. He never cares about the headlines. I said to him, 'Well go ahead and buy me that paper.' Of course, it didn't have any names in it. Then we headed out to my dad's in Covina. While there, my dad and I got into a discussion about how many had been killed. I think it was around 513 (deaths) at that time. Normally we would visit with my dad for a couple hours then go home but this time I thought, 'Why don't we go to the movies?' so we did.

We arrived home about ten o'clock that night after the longer than usual visit with my father. When we turned down our street we noticed a vehicle with a government license plate parked in front of our house. My first thought was, 'Did Jason make a surprise visit and get to come home or something?' Then Mitch said, 'Well, there's somebody in the car' as we drove by it to pull into our driveway. I kept watching them as we pulled into the driveway then I saw them get out and put their jackets on. When they got to the car they said, 'We're looking for Gail Farnsworth.' Mitch said, 'This is she.' They really wouldn't talk to him and they came to me and said, 'Are you Gail Farnsworth?' All I could say at that point was, 'Oh my God! Oh my God! Oh my God!' Then they said, 'Can we go inside?' I kept saying the same thing, 'Oh my God! Oh my God! Oh my God!' When we were in the house they told me that there were three of them walking back from their post to their vehicle just getting off duty and a car drove up beside them and detonated. Jason was 22 years and 23 days old on the 24th."

Sunday, January 24, 2004 was a routine typical day in Iraq. On the bridge crossing the Euphrates River the citizens were very common and unsuspicious as they passed the checkpoint in their vehicles, just like any other day when one shift ended the next began. It was mid-day when the next group of soldiers arrived. Upon their entry Jason's unit began its preparations for departure. Spc. Joshua Johnson, the medic assigned to the unit said,

"I was looking for a place to catch a ride. Chappell, Sturges and Rosenberg offered me a ride in their Humvee, but my medic bag was in a different Humvee and I'm not supposed to part with my bag, so I rode in the vehicle that had my bag. We were in a convoy of seven vehicles and I was in the third one. Chappell was the driver in the second one. We were just driving away from our post. We had not left yet. We were just lining up and getting ready to head out over the bridge and go back to our base. The Humvee I was in was lagging about 20 to 30 feet behind Chappell's. I was sitting in the passenger seat behind the driver and I remember hearing Baker, the machine gun operator on our Humvee, yell out, 'Oh shit!' I remember the explosion then I blacked out for a few seconds. I think I was knocked unconscious for a moment. The front windows in our Humvee were blown out so the concussion really dazed me.

An orange and white 2-door hatchback, which is a standard taxi in Iraq, rammed into the driver's side of Chappell's Humvee and detonated at the same time. This suicide driver knew when our shift change was and came across the bridge at that time. He was able to make it through the check point quick and uncontested. It was quick. The blast flipped Chappell's Humvee over and blew it into a field. Just the frame was left. All four wheels were gone. Chappell, Sturges and Rosenberg were ejected and landed about fifty feet from the vehicle. I was told that Rosenberg had a pulse but I couldn't find one. Chappell and Sturges were killed instantly. The suicide vehicle disintegrated. There was nothing left from it. I was told later that the blast was equivalent to two thousand pounds of TNT."

The Department of Defense's Immediate Release read:

The Department of Defense announced today the death of three soldiers who were supporting Operation Iraqi Freedom. Three Task Force "All American" soldiers were killed when a vehicle-based improvised explosive device detonated in Khalidiyah, Iraq, Jan. 24. Killed were:

Spc. Jason K. Chappell, 22, of Hemet, Calif.
Spc. William R. Sturges Jr., 24, of Spring Church, Pa.
Sgt. Randy S. Rosenberg, 23, of Berlin, N.H.
The soldiers were assigned to Company B, 1st Squadron, 9th Cavalry, Fort Hood Texas.

The incident is under investigation.

These three individuals gave the highest act of valor one has to offer his country. But even being a hero in the eyes of a grateful nation cannot curb the shock that devastated their families. In an instant, their relatives were forced to experience the burden of freedom first hand. It is a unique pain that only family members can understand and they pray it will not last forever, but unfortunately the effects are permanent.

Jason's mother Gail said,

"I stay away from these groups that have the welcome home parties. It's not because I'm not thankful they are coming home. It's because mine didn't and it's very hard on me. I don't know if that's selfishness or not. It's not that I wish something would happen to them, Lord knows I would never want anything to happen to them. I just don't want to be reminded that my son is never coming home and I don't know if I ever will want to be reminded. His birthday is New Year's Day, so every New Year is hard. I quit celebrating holidays because it's just easier that way.

I also have guilt because I'm not much of a letter writer and I didn't write him right away. I was giving most of my attention to my daughter who was still in school. I also was struggling with the effects of a mild stroke I had about one year before we lost Jason. The stroke kept me from work so we were also dealing with financial issues at the time and when I finally wrote him through email he really reamed me for taking so long. He seemed so angry at me. I sent a letter explaining things to him. I also thought we could clear it up when he got back home because you never think anything like this is going to happen. I never got the chance to clear it up with him and he never got the chance to read the last letter I sent to him."

Jason's widow Stephanie has had her struggles. She said,

"February 4, 2004 was his funeral and once you lose your spouse the Army gives you 90 days to move off base. The other Army wives were like family to me so in this short period of time I felt like I lost two parts of my family. I understand the Army needs the space to move another family on base, but it just didn't seem right to me that I was forced to lose two parts of my family at once.

I only had 18 months with Jason, and he was the last of the Chappells. One year after his funeral my niece was born, and her middle name is Chappell.

In June 2011 I was sitting in an economics course when my professor started talking about our defense spending basically being a waste of time and resources and insinuating that our military bullies people. I stood up and said, 'I'm sorry but if you're going to stand there and bash the country that my husband died for, I'm not going to sit here and listen to you.' And I walked out.

It doesn't get any easier. You just learn how to live with it. I'm so focused on being Jason's widow that I feel guilty for trying to love somebody else, and this is eight years later (2012)."

Chapter 2
The Spirit of Bravery

"Heroes rise from the tumult of war, but for every hero there are casualties."

— *Forrest Haggerty*

There is no concern for one's self when the spirit of bravery directs an individual's actions in moments of deadly circumstances. The only wish for the brave one is to protect their family, comrades, or brothers in arms. Extraordinary actions have been recorded throughout history when individuals thrust themselves into harm's way in order to protect others. First Lieutenant Rick Posselt walked into a hail storm of bullets to pull out a mortally wounded comrade in Haditha, Iraq.

Haditha, Iraq was a gathering spot for insurgents beginning in 2003. In 2004, after the U.S. Marines left the local police in charge of the city, insurgents rounded up about 20 of the police officers and executed them on the soccer field in the middle of Haditha. It was a successful attempt to strike terror in the minds of the locals who were thinking about collaborating with the U.S. military. By 2005 the insurgents controlled the town with Taliban type rules. Previous infrequent visits by U.S. forces allowed insurgents to gain a strangle hold on the town's people and leadership. On May 24, 2005 Operation New Market was launched by the U.S. military in an effort to eventually remove the insurgency. On August 1, 2005 six U.S. Marines were killed in an ambush and two days later, on August 3rd, 14 more Marines were killed in an IED explosion potentially causing a rise in tensions between U.S. Forces and the insurgency. On November 19, 12 Marines from the 3rd Battalion, 1st Marines engaged in a fire fight and ended up killing 24 Iraqi civilians, 11 of which were women and children. This incident stirred a controversy alleging that the killings were in retribution for the killing of Lance Corporal Miguel Terrazas who was killed by an IED earlier in the day. This incident came to be known as the "Haditha Killings" that had political ramifications, which caused the 3rd Battalion, 1st Marines to be replaced with the 3rd Battalion, 3rd Marines in March of 2006.

The 3/3 Marines tactics were to saturate the streets with perambulating units and motorized units. Twenty-four hours a day seven days a week the streets of Haditha were inundated with U.S. and allied patrols in an attempt to subdue, contain, and capture the insurgents.

June 14, 2006

First Lieutenant Rick Posselt and his unit from India Company were on patrol in the streets of Haditha on an intelligence gathering mission. They were looking for a person of importance to question. India Company's commanding officer, Capt. Andy Lynch, was one block over with his unit also gathering intelligence on this individual. Captain Lynch said:

> "I was in a house one block over talking to a former Iraqi police officer and through an interpreter he was telling me how the current generation of Iraqis had no respect for the law when I heard a shot followed by an eruption of gun fire. Then I heard on the radio, 'We have a man down, urgent surgical.' Our triage system has four categories for sorting injuries: Routine, Priority, Urgent, and Urgent Surgical, so when I heard 'Urgent Surgical' I knew we had a serious injury on our hands, because that's the worst one, the most serious."

1st Lt. Posselt's patrol was comprised of 4 Marines, Posselt, Cpl. Michael Estrella, Lcpl. Brian Thomas, Sgt Jason Sakowski and 6 members of the Iraqi Army. Sgt. Jason Sakowski said,

> "We did what is called satellite patrolling. Satellite patrolling is when the squad splits in two or three groups so one, the enemy can't tell where everyone is and two, they don't know the true number of our force.
> We split into two groups. Lt. Posselt, Cpl. Estrella and three Iraqi soldiers went East. Cpl. Estrella was the head of all communications and he was carrying the main radio. I had the secondary radio if we were ever to lose communication with the main radio.

My team, which was made up of Lcpl. Thomas, three Iraqi Soldiers and myself hung back on the main road leading away from the FOB (Forward Operation Base) in a North East direction. Our plan was to meet at a particular intersection and regroup.

As my group walked east down a road lined with shops Lt. Posselt's group crossed the road about 100 yards ahead of us. They were heading north, from our right to our left. Lt. Posselt was in the lead and Cpl. Estrella was a few feet behind him. The Iraqi soldiers were a few feet behind Cpl. Estrella. When Cpl. Estrella was in the middle of the intersection that's when the shot rang out. I watched him fall to the ground like he just got knocked out and I actually thought he was hit in the leg by the way he went down. Everyone started returning fire toward the insurgents. Lt. Posselt immediately grabbed Estrella and started dragging him to the closest building to provide protection for him. Lt. Posselt did it under heavy enemy fire. It was very hot that day and the tar roads got very hot and soft, so all the rounds hitting around him were tearing up the road around him. There were so many enemy bullets hitting around him. There were too many to count.

After I fired a couple of rounds, Lcpl. Thomas and I ducked into a small shop nearby so I could start sending a casualty report and request a Quick Reaction Force (QRF) and Medevac with the second radio.

After about five minutes of engaging the enemy the QRF showed up and quarantined the area and started searching for insurgents from where the gunfire was coming. At this point Lcpl Thomas and I linked up with Lt. Posselt at the casualty collection point and we started taking Estrella's gear off so he could be put into the Humvee and transported to the Medevac air field.

I can remember us using whatever water we had on us to clean the blood from the floor so none of the insurgents could see that they had taken one of us."

About this time Captain Lynch arrived on the scene. He said,

"When we finally made it over to the location they had Cpl. Estrella laying on a table inside one of the shops and all his gear had been taken off.

> He had a single gunshot wound on his neck near the base of his skull and yet he was still alive. He was still breathing."

The team had walked into an ambush that was well coordinated with fire coming from the front and crossfire coming from a ninety degree angle off to their right about 200 yards. The ambush was initiated with a single sniper shot from the front that struck Cpl. Estrella high on the left side of his neck. Cpl. Michael Estrella was placed on the Humvee and transported to the Medvac airfield.

With it being his third tour of duty, and having never lost a comrade to death, Sgt. Sakowski said,

> "The movement back to base was a very sad one. I had been in a lot of firefights where people got wounded, but they had never involved a Marine dying. I suddenly lost my feeling of invincibility. We left the wire with 10 packs and it really hit me hard when I called into the COC and gave them our head count of 9 packs entering the wire.
>
> Cpl. Estrella was asked to go on the mission because we were short one Marine for the patrol. Estrella was the Commanding Officer's radioman and the head of all communications for the FOB and only went out with the CO on missions. He normally did not leave the wire for routine patrols from the FOB. I believe Thomas asked him to join our patrol to help out because they were friends.
>
> I remember us having sweet and sour chicken for dinner before getting ready for that mission. I have not eaten sweet and sour chicken since that day.
>
> After we got back on base we did a debriefing of what happened and then we were told to get some rest. The next day I had a mission at zero dark thirty as if nothing ever happened the day before. The daily grind of patrolling and firefights never stopped on that deployment."

A fearless Lt. Posselt pulled Cpl. Estrella approximately five meters to safety in a hail storm of enemy bullets. Other marines who witnessed it said it was the bravest action they had ever seen. In an article submitted by Regimental Combat Team 7 shortly after the incident Sgt. Jason Sakowski was quoted as saying,

"This is my third combat deployment, but it is the first time I have seen bravery to that degree."

According to the same article, also present at the time of the incident was an Iraqi soldier named Muhammad. He was assigned to the 2nd Battalion, 2nd Brigade, 7th Iraqi Army Division and through an interpreter he said,

"He showed uncommon courage that day. He set an example for other soldiers to follow. I think he is a hero."

Even though he is being hailed as a hero, Lieutenant Posselt sees things differently. In the same Regimental Combat Team 7 article Posselt was quoted as saying,

". . .when I knew he was injured, the first thing I thought of was -- I have to get him to safety. That's all that was going through my head.. . . any other Marine . . . would have done the same thing that day. I just happened to be the Marine closest to Estrella when he fell. I had to get him off that street and that was really the only thought going through my mind. I just did what my instinct told me to do. I was just trying to take care of my Marines. I am not the Marine who deserves the recognition. Cpl. Michael Estrella is the real hero and deserves the recognition."

Lieutenant Posselt was awarded the Bronze Star with V for his actions and has been hailed as a hero for his bravery, but for every hero there are casualties. Unfortunately, 20-year-old Cpl. Michael Estrella would succumb to his wound and pass away on the helicopter en route to the hospital leaving behind a heartbroken and devastated family.

Cpl. Michael Anthony Estrella

Chapter 3
Cpl. Michael Anthony Estrella

A year and a half after losing Jason Chappell the town of Hemet, California, would receive news of Michael Estrella's death. Michael would be the 2,500th American killed in Iraq.

Jessica Estrella, one of Michael's younger sisters, wrote,

"I was in my house when I heard the doorbell ring. I opened the door not knowing who it would be and there stood two Marines and one Navy soldier. I didn't think anything of it until I saw a red 4 to 5-inch folder in the hands of one of the Marines, and right then and there I knew something bad had happened to my brother.

One of the Marines asked me to call my mom and I really didn't want to call her and make her day a living hell, but I had no choice."

Michael's Mother Maria said,

"I will never forget that day I received the frantic call at work from my daughter Jessica. She was home alone when the Marines and Navy rang the doorbell. They wouldn't say anything to her until the whole family was together. After her phone call I was unable to move and everything was moving in slow motion. I called my husband and told him that the Marines were at our door. He was driving Michael's car that day and later he told me that was the most horrible ride he ever made. The anticipation was killing him. I knew why they were there. I was just hoping they would tell me my son was hurt and I needed to go with them to see him.

One of my co-workers drove me home. It felt like I would never make it home."

Jessica wrote,

"One of the Marines took me to pick up my three youngest siblings from school. I didn't know what to expect when they stepped into the car. My two little brothers and little sister kept asking me what was going on. I sat there and said, 'nothing.' I just sat there in silence and cried trying not to let them see me crying.

Once we got home I walked into the house and saw my mom and dad sitting down together. My mom was bawling out tears as she looked at us. When I saw her, I cried even more knowing my brother wasn't with us anymore. We all sat in the living room as a family and I heard the Marine say 'I'm sorry for your loss.' He was trying not to cry.

I felt like there was going to be no tomorrow after he said that. My 6-year-old brother didn't understand what was going on until my mom told him. I remember him saying 'Why is Michael dead?' I cried and cried knowing he will be asking for a long time until he understood that his older brother was killed in Iraq."

Michael Anthony Estrella, born August 25, 1985 in Santa Ana, California, was the eldest of six children. The Marines who came to his parent's home would not say a word until all five of his younger siblings and his parents were in the room.

Michael volunteered to join the Marine Corps in August of 2003 after thoroughly enjoying four years of high school ROTC at Hemet High School. Not even the thought of being sent to war would hinder his passion for honorably serving his country.

At the conclusion of his basic training he was placed with India Company, 3rd battalion, 3rd Marines regimental combat team based in Hawaii at the Kaneohe Bay Marine Corp base. The unit was deployed to Hadithah, Iraq in March 2006 to carry out their job of counter-insurgency, (COIN), or seeking out the enemy. Iraq was Michael's second tour of duty. His first was in 2004 when India Company, 3/3 Marines was sent to Kunar, Afghanistan, to carry out the same counter-insurgency task as well as provide security for the Provincial Reconstruction Team and help the locals with what they needed, which was mostly medical attention. Michael was a radio operator and his company commander Lieutenant Colonel Jim Sweeney spoke highly about Michael's physical and mental resilience:

> "He went everywhere with me carrying at least one radio on his back, sometimes two. They were heavy and I would ask him if he needed help and he always said, 'No.' He was tough. He never complained. He was an all-around solid Marine and if it were possible I would seek him out today to serve alongside him again."

Iraq's relatively flat desert setting is a stark contrast to the geography of the steep, lush green, mountainous terrain in the Kunar Province of Afghanistan. Except for the Euphrates River which provides life to the green farmland and foliage along its banks, Hadithah is a relatively dry, visually drab, and dusty farming town that is typical of a third-world nation. It is made mostly of dirt roads lined with grimy residential dwellings and businesses that suffered from the 2003 infestation of insurgents. As one of several hot spots for insurgents, Michael and his unit were sent there with the task of removing these insurrectionary individuals. An arduous task but not strenuous enough to deter Michael's drive to fulfill his duty along with the team he was a part of. However, misfortune would find Michael that awful day in June 2006 and his family would be left to deal with the repercussions.

Second guessing one's actions is a very common response for parents who have lost a child. Intuitively they may always feel as if there was something they could have done to prevent their horrible loss. Feeling responsible for her son's passing, Maria blames herself for not doing more to save him. The emotion of guilt has caused her to think about things she could have done to intervene:

> "I have always felt that this was my entire fault. I had just spoken to Michael that weekend three times in one day. The third call that day we were joking around. I was going to run an errand but I thought to myself I could do that later because this might be my last call. All the other calls that day ended with "I love you," but this last one we just said, "good-bye." I look back and remember that when I said good-bye there was a silence on both ends. That was the last words I heard from my son. I know that Michael always knew that I love him, but I just want to scream out to him and let him know. If only I can have that moment back to tell him that I love him
>
> He called me to ask me for grandpa's number. He was worried because his great-grandfather was dying of cancer. He wanted to come home to see him.

He asked me to put out a Red Cross alert so he could come home and visit him. I called the Red Cross but since Grandpa was not his immediate family they did not send it. Michael again asked for me to call them and let them know that by law no matter who it is they need to send out an alert. I told Michael that his grandfather was doing better but as soon as we get the word that he is not doing well I would call the Red Cross again. I did not get that chance. If I had done what my son asked me to do maybe Michael would be here with us now. I know this is my fault because Michael wanted to come home and I did not listen. I will never forgive myself for not protecting my child and making that call."

The pressure, strain and anxiety from the traumatic experience can carry unpleasant physical repercussions on loved ones. For Maria, it was a loss of appetite.

"I was not able to eat after receiving the news of his passing. I just felt very sick to my stomach. Any food I could smell or look at just made me sick. I could not eat for almost two weeks and I lost ten pounds."

The grieving process is a burden for each individual, and all cope with it differently. The shock from the dreadful news of losing a child can be too overwhelming to completely digest, and denial is a typical beginning symptom. However, it is a necessary natural defense system which allows loved ones to absorb such a huge loss at their own rate. Maria said:

"All I could do was sit on the couch and stare at the door hoping Michael would walk through it. I would sit and wait for his phone call just so I could hear him say it was all a bad joke.

It took several months to receive all of his belongings. Some came from Hawaii. Some came from Iraq and some came from his friends. It became increasingly difficult to receive his belongings knowing he would never use them again. I said to my husband, 'Why are we receiving his things when he should be bringing them home himself?'

I kept his things in our living room for nearly a year and I would not allow anyone to touch his belongings. I just kept thinking I would leave them there, and one day he would come home and tell me it was all a big joke. I would just sit in the living room and go through his things. Some would make me cry, and some would make me laugh. His computer had his homemade videos of him and his friends. On his videos, he is laughing and joking like he always had. Even though it hurts to see him, hear him, and not be able to touch him I am grateful he made these videos so I can go back and see the way he was.

We have had family members ask us why we keep his things. They have also asked if we are going to give his things away. Most people do not seem to understand what it means to have his belongings. They do not appreciate how precious his shoes are to us or how his shirts smell or what it means to take care of his car. I sometimes feel like he will still be sitting there when I look for him. I have been told that some people can't come to my home because I have his pictures up. I will never take his pictures down. He is a part of my family and he will always be. If they cannot accept that I have his pictures up then they are not welcomed in my home.

Sometimes the only way I can wake up and make it through my day is by thinking Michael is still in Iraq. I still wait for his call or for him to walk through the front door. The other day I was in my hallway and I felt as if Michael was in the house. I called out to him. My husband just stared at me and asked if I was okay. My kids just stayed quiet and I could see their eyes water up. I thought he would come to me or answer me. But it never happened. Afterward I sat on my couch and cried. My son Nathan came up to me the next day very upset and said, 'Why did you call out to Michael?' I did not know how to respond. I can still hear him calling me and laughing. I can still hear his voice."

Many troops in battle have spoken about the 'Law of Averages,' which implies that if they make it through one campaign unscathed their chances of making it through the next crusade narrows and they feel the odds of becoming a casualty will increase. Of course, there is no mathematical equation proving this theory, but there is an intuitive gut feeling that some of these warriors cannot ignore or deny. A sensation deep within their soul tells them that something bad is going to happen and unfortunately when a warrior has this particular gut feeling it tends to be right more times than it is wrong. As if it were a date with destiny, their fate is unfurled before their minds' eyes just prior to it becoming a reality.

At home Michael never spoke of this deep seeded knowledge of fate, but his actions showed his mother that he knew more than he let on. Maria said:

> "Looking back, I now know that Michael knew he was not coming home. There were just too many things he did different that he had never done any other time. One thing he did was ship his car home from Hawaii. He usually would leave it with a friend in Hawaii when he was deployed. This time he sent it home and gave me the power of attorney. He also had everything very organized. When I began receiving some of his belongings from Iraq I went through his daily notebook and saw that he wrote down everything he needed to prepare before he left. These were things he normally did not do.
>
> In the past, when he was at home on leave he would go spend time with his girlfriend or hang out with his friends, but this time he just wanted to spend time with his family. When I was at work and the kids were in school Michael would go to work with his dad in the family business. I would say, 'You should stay home and rest.' He would say, 'No, I just want to spend time with Dad.'
>
> The last time Michael was home on his two-week leave he was not himself. He seemed very depressed and scared. I could see that Michael was not well so I told him I would talk to his sergeant or commander so he would not have to go to Iraq. He said, 'No matter what I need to go be with my brothers. I can't let them down as they would never let me down and if something happens to me that is what God wants.' Michael just looked very sad.
>
> All the kids were close to Michael especially Nathan (the youngest of the kids). He seemed to have a deeper connection with Michael because every time he would call Nathan would know it was Michael before the phone was answered.

> "Two weeks prior to Michael's passing Nathan came up to my husband and told him that Michael was dead. Immediately my husband was upset and told Nathan not to say that. Later in the week when Michael called home I told him what Nathan said. Michael was quiet for a moment and then he said that something almost happened to him. I believe Nathan had a premonition of what was going to happen."

What almost happened to Michael was an IED struck a vehicle in a convoy he was a part of.

Watching kids develop is usually a process all parents plan to take pleasure in. We expect to see our children grow into adults and begin a family of their own, perhaps with the wonder of what our in-laws and grandchildren might be like. These expectations can usually be anticipated because they fit in with the natural flow of human subsistence and the perpetuation of family lineage. In most cases, it is simply taken for granted that we will experience such a pleasure and do not imagine any other outcome except for what we imagine in our hopes, expectations, and dreams for our children. We may just assume that eventually we will experience this God-given blessing. Michael's parents were no different. They planned on experiencing their firstborn child's transition into responsible adulthood and parenthood, because that is what he was planning on doing. Maria said:

> "He wanted to become an officer with the SWAT team and start a family. One thing he told me just before he left was that he wanted a child. His life had hardly begun and he did not get the chance to fulfill his dream. My son will never get a chance to have children. It hurts me to think that I was not there to protect him so he could have lived a full life. He was supposed to live a long and happy life. He never gave us any problems. He was the type of person that if you needed help he would stop whatever he was doing to give you a hand. He never thought about himself first. He always made sure everyone else was taken care of before him. No matter what was going on around him he was always smiling

and laughing. If he was sick, not feeling well, or sad, he would just keep on laughing.

This has all been hard on my family and I still don't know how I get out of bed in the morning. I miss my son more than anything."

Michael's viewing took place on the evening of June 22, 2006. With so many mourners wanting to pay their respects the viewing ran an hour over its scheduled finish time of 9:00 p.m. Maria said:

"On the evening of Michael's viewing I just wanted to spend time with him. I was so focused on my son that I had not noticed a single person until it was time to leave. The line was huge. It was comforting to know so many people cared, but still heartbreaking."

Michael was laid to rest on Friday, June 23, 2006 at Riverside National Cemetery in Riverside, California. Approximately one thousand people attended his service. The procession of vehicles following Michael to the cemetery was nearly a mile and a half long. With every seat filled at the memorial park's largest auditorium there was standing room only. Maria said:

"I was touched, honored, and it was comforting. More importantly, I was grateful so many people cared about Michael.

I was looking at my son's enlistment papers, and 2007 would have been his last year in the Marine Corp. I have many questions that I know will never be answered. People say things happen for a reason, but what reason was there for my son to die?

One day while I was at a gas station a man walked up to me and asked me if the name on the truck was my husband. I said, 'No, it is my son's.' Immediately the man said, 'Your husband is right. You will see your son again.' I had no idea who this man was nor had I ever seen him before, therefore, it was impossible for him to know that a week before this experience my husband told me that we would see Michael again. I don't know if that was a sign from Michael, but I like to think it was."

Michael received the Purple Heart, the Combat Action Ribbon, the National Defense Service Medal, the Afghanistan Campaign Medal, the Iraqi Campaign Medal, the Global War on Terrorism Service Medal, and the Sea Service Deployment Ribbon with the Bronze Star. Michael also received the Hawaii Medal of Honor in May of 2007. His mother said:

> "I would have loved for him to receive these medals himself. He would have been very proud and excited. But instead, I received them for him. I miss my son with all of my heart and I am proud and honored to say that I had the privilege to be his mom."

October 2006

Four months after Michael's passing the residents of Hemet would hear of their third loss:Army Cpl. Kenny Francis Stanton Jr., who graduated from Hemet High School in 2004, one year after Michael Estrella graduated.

Cpl. Michael Anthony Estrella

Michael in a photo collage his mother Maria put together.
The photo on the lower left is Michael with his two younger brothers
shortly before his final deployment.

Cpl. Kenny Francis Stanton Jr.

Chapter 4
Cpl. Kenny Francis Stanton Jr.

After Kenny's initial attempt failed to get him into the Army, due to childhood asthma and seizures, his second attempt proved successful when he did not list his past ailments, because he had grown out of them years before.

Kenny enlisted for five years and was assigned to the 57th Military Police Company, Waegwan, Korea after completing basic training. He arrived in Iraq in July 2006, and sixteen days after his 20th birthday he would lose his life from an IED that detonated near the Humvee he was riding in on October 13, 2006 in Baghdad, Iraq.

A lover of poetry, reading, and writing, Kenny's plan was to go to college and become an English teacher back at Hemet High School after he completed his military service. While a student at Hemet High he had a monthly column in the school newspaper titled, "Ask Kenny." According to an article written in the *L.A. Times* on October 22, 2006, his dad said that Kenny ". . . hoped to start classes once he completed his one-year tour in Iraq and shipped out to Hawaii for the remainder of his five-year enlistment." In the same article, his friend Paul described Kenny as ". . . open to new experiences, always liking to meet new people, and he always had a smile." Paul referred to Kenny as his "brother from another mother".

The community of Hemet was stunned by the tragic news of losing their third local boy in two years and the sentiments of the town were pretty much summed up in a phrase by one of his friends that was posted on Kenny's MySpace account that read, "The Plague that Hit Hemet." Kenny's youngest sister, Terrymarie Stanton said,

"On that morning, I woke up and I don't know why, but I had this feeling to get up and go to the door. As I walked into the hallway I saw my mother standing by the door. There was somebody in uniform walking up to the door from outside. He hadn't even knocked yet and all of us were there. It was as if we all felt it. My mother answered the door and the first thing she said was, "Well this can't be good news, because it's early." He didn't say anything. He took off his hat and asked if he could have a moment to speak with us and if we could all sit down. My mother and father sat on the couch. Me and my brother Mario also sat on the couch. My sister Brandie was standing behind us. Then, he told us that on October 13th my brother had passed away.

I remember him saying it was during active duty that a "Road Side Bomb" had hit his Humvee and he wasn't able to make it out. I remember him saying there were others in the vehicle and they all made it out, but my brother was the only one who lost his life."

Kenny's death took a heavy toll on his family. Kenny's sister shared the harsh reality that the burden of freedom can have on a family.

Terrymarie said,

"After my brother died we weren't the same after that. We all became unglued, and we all dealt with it differently.

My brother Mario has never been the same. He never opened up again. He seemed to go inside himself and not come out. He can't talk about it, and he can't even go to the burial site. He can make it to the cemetery, but he can't go up to the headstone. He just can't make it that far.

My sister Brandie went into shock when she found out about it and she showed no emotions. She went completely into shock with a blank look on her face until the day of his funeral when he was lowered into the ground. That's when she was finally able to let it out. Like the whole family, she took it very hard.

My mother became more fearful about the rest of her children. One time my sister talked to her about death and my mother lost it. She said, 'You're not going! I cannot lose another child! A mother is never supposed to bury her children!'

My father dealt with it by drinking, and he just lost it. He developed a bad drinking habit. My parents separated and never got back together. My family just broke apart."

While Kenny was in the military, he formed bonds with other soldiers that he met while on active duty.

Terrymarie said,

"My brother was a part of a group who called themselves "The Four Brothers." I spoke with one of the Four Brothers several years after my brother passed away, and he informed me that some of the members from that little group had also died in the war. Since then I have lost contact with him."

On October 16, 2006, The Department of Defense posted the following on their "Immediate Release" statement:

> *The Department of Defense announced today the death of a soldier who was supporting Operation Iraqi Freedom.*
>
> *Pfc. Kenny F. Stanton Jr., 20, of Hemet, Calif.,*
>
> *died on Oct. 13 in Baghdad, Iraq, from injuries suffered when an improvised explosive device detonated near his vehicle.*
>
> *Stanton was assigned to the 57th Military Police Company, Waegwan, Korea.*

Kenny was laid to rest on October 23, 2006 in a Christian funeral service that began at 10:00 a.m. in Hemet, California at Our Lady of the Valley Catholic Church. After the church service the procession drove the 25 miles to Riverside National Cemetery for Kenny's final burial. During the funeral, Hemet resident, Charles "Ed" Sare, was on his lunch break. He said:

> "I was coming home from work for lunch and when I turned down my street I noticed a military van parked across the street from my house. I pulled into my drive way and stepped out of my car. When I looked back at the van the three guys inside were walking across the street toward me, and as they approached me I said, 'I hope you're not here to tell me what I think you're going to tell me.' And one of them said, 'Yes sir, we are.'"

Ed's oldest son, Charles Otto Sare, would be the fourth Hemet boy to give the ultimate sacrifice.

Cpl. Kenny Francis Stanton Jr.

HN. Charles Otto Sare

Chapter 5
HN. Charles Otto Sare

"He believed in the mission. That's why he wanted to go."
— Charles "Ed" Sare, father.

Charles Otto Sare, nicknamed "Otter," was born on December 3, 1982 at Hemet Hospital in Hemet, California. He was the firstborn to Charles Edwin Sare and Victoria Lynette Sare. When the doctors saw that he was in a breech position a cesarean was performed and Otter came into the world a healthy baby boy. On November 15, 1984, his younger brother Matthew was born. Otter and Matthew would be the only children the Sares would have. According to his dad Otter was a perfect baby that never had any health issues, with the exception of hernia surgery at the age of 18 months.

When Otter was nine months old his father took him to Glamis, California, put him in his baby backpack and rode him through the desert on his quad. Otter would come to love it so much that Ed bought Otter his first quad for Christmas when Otter was four years old. Eventually, going out to Glamis with his quad would become a favorite past time for Otter.

The Sare family was living in Homeland, California at the time. Homeland is located approximately 10 miles west of Hemet, and it is a rural ranch country where the homes have larger plots of land. When Otter was 4 years old he walked into his house alone and his mother asked him where Matt was. Otter answered with, "I don't know." His mother decided to go outside and look for Matt. After a short search, Vikki found Matt sitting inside a rabbit cage. Otter talked his 2-year-old brother into crawling inside then locked the cage and walked away. Matt was found sitting in the cage with a smile on his face.

Growing up, Otter participated in various sports such as soccer and basketball through Valley Wide Recreation and played baseball through Hemet Youth. Baseball was his favorite of the sports, so he continued with baseball through Valley Wide Recreation until he was too old to play. Otter became such a good baseball player that other kids always wanted to be on his team. He played all positions successfully. He could play outfield, any in field position, and pitcher. Otter's father remembered a specific incident when Otter hit a foul ball into the stands and it broke the nose of a woman not paying attention.

In 1992, Otter's parents separated. It was at this point that Ed made it a tradition to take his boys out to White Water, California every New Year to ride their quads in the desert. It was a tradition that lasted until the late '90s.

When Otter was 13 years old he learned to drive his dad's Jeep in the San Jacinto riverbed in San Jacinto, California. One day, while driving in the riverbed, Ed put Otter in the driver's seat and instructed him through the process. He loved it. In fact, Otter loved it so much that when he was older he would frequently visit the place in his own vehicle and drive the riverbed for hours. Sometimes he would do this with friends, and sometimes alone.

Otter was also a typical boy with typical mishaps. At the age of 13 he and a friend made their own fishing lures. The lures had a three-prong hook on each end. When they were finished, Otter decided to take his lure home to show his dad, so he placed it in his right front pocket and walked home. By the time he made it home, he was limping. His father asked him why he was limping and he explained that he put the lure in his pocket and one of the hooks had hooked him. When Ed looked, he could see it was only an inch or two from his privates. He could also see that the barb was too far below the surface of the skin for him to pull out. So, he told Otter the only way to get it out was to push it all the way through. After cutting the eye of the hook off with pliers Ed said, "Are you ready?" Otter said, "Yes." Ed pushed it through and removed it from his groin. Otter never put hooks in his pocket again.

Two years later, at the age of 15, Otter came home again with a funny walk and a banged-up face. He said to his dad, "I think I broke my balls." Ed asked him what happened, and he said he was jumping his BMX bike over some dirt jumps. On one of the jumps his feet slipped off the pedals and he landed, very hard, on the seat. It sent him over the handlebars and he landed on his face. Once again, Ed had him pull down his pants to check. He noticed an ample amount of blood in his underwear. After Otter cleaned himself off they both could see there was only a small laceration that spread blood making it appear worse than it actually was.

While in high school Otter thoroughly enjoyed the Future Farmers of America (FFA). Raising animals and taking them to the fair was something he took great pleasure in. Otter's dad said that Otter enjoyed the fairs, because they would get him out of school for the day.

Otter's entire public education took place in the Hemet Unified School District, and he would eventually graduate from Hemet High School with the class of 2001. His first job was at Stater Brother's Market for a short while. After that he began working for America's Tire Store. Both stores were in Hemet.

Everywhere he went he made friends effortlessly. Many people who met him said they would hit it off with him right away, and everybody who knew Otter said he was the type of person who wanted people to feel good. If Otter crossed paths with someone who was having a bad day, he would not leave them alone until he got them to smile.

While he was in high school he would go out of his way to give a hand to the special needs students. He was always helpful, and respectful to those students. If anybody else made fun of them he was quick to defend them and put the antagonizing individual in his or her place. This compassion was not limited to just people. One night in 2003, while driving, Otter swerved off the road and ended up rolling his truck twice as a result of avoiding a coyote that crossed the road. Miraculously, he was unscathed, but his truck was totaled, and the coyote was fine.

In November of 2004, Otter was sent to North Chicago, Illinois to the Recruit Training Command (RTC) known as the boot camp for the Navy. About two years after graduating high school Otter decided he wanted to be a paramedic. He figured his best bet for medical training was through the military. He had a love for children and a love for people. According to his dad, helping the sick and injured was something he considered to be a "sacred trust."

Upon completion of his basic training, Otter was sent to Field Medical School at Camp Pendleton, California. It was at Camp Pendleton that he completed over 378 hours of medical field training, survival skills, and several other necessary services to become a hospitalman. From Camp Pendleton, he was sent to the Naval Ambulatory clinic in Port Hueneme, California, a clinic that provides medical and dental care to active duty personnel and their families. This was something Otter thoroughly enjoyed while gaining valuable knowledge and experience for his future profession.

Otter's dad would eventually remarry in March 2006 to Karen Waterman, whom he met through Genesis Construction where they were both employed. Karen was a project specialist, and Charles was an equipment mechanic. Karen had three children: Prince, Chaz, and Schuyler (pronounced Skyler). Since Otter loved children he would take Schuyler to Dairy Queen for ice cream. Sometimes he would take him to the local am pm mini-mart and buy him a slushy and sour Skittles. Afterwards he would take Schuyler back home and turn him loose with a sugar high. Karen and Charles would then get to watch Schuyler "bounce off the walls." Otter would get a good laugh out of it.

On one occasion, when Schuyler was seven, Otter took him to his friend Brandon's house. Before they arrived, Otter paid Schuyler five dollars to randomly kick Brandon in the shins throughout the night. Brandon ended up with sore shins.

In September 2006, while in Port Hueneme, California, 6'3" Otter was chosen to go to Iraq by his superior Chief Martinez. Otter called home and informed his father that he would be going to Iraq. He arrived there in September. He was assigned to the 3rd Battalion, 4th Marine Regiment, 1st Marine Division. They were stationed next to the Syrian border at camp Tarawa in Al Qaim in the Al Anbar Province.

On the night of October 23, 2006, the four-vehicle convoy Otter was a part of was out on a security patrol. Different convoys would patrol at various times to maintain a presence in the town. While heading back to base camp they were driving down a dirt road approximately 12 to 15 feet wide. Walls roughly six to eight feet high lined both sides of the road. At about 9:06 p.m., when they were approximately one mile from base camp, the convoy encountered an IED. The alternate commander of the convoy was Cpl. Thomas Katakowski. He said:

"It was the first patrol of four scheduled for that night. We were heading east on a narrow road that seemed like an alleyway in the neighborhood. I was the front seat passenger in the fourth vehicle. As we were driving along I saw an explosion about a hundred feet in front of us. I could see the vehicle it hit get lifted about six feet straight up with flames all around it. It was high enough to where it was lifted above the vehicle that was about fifty feet in front of us. I assumed it was the first vehicle. We immediately stopped, pushed our vehicle back, and faced it to the west to set up security. I told my driver to call in that we got hit. I could see there was a fire so I grabbed the fire extinguisher in our vehicle and headed to the sight.

When I arrived, I realized it was the second vehicle, because Cpl. Toliver was standing there with his extinguisher and he was the driver of the lead vehicle. I saw that Shaw, the driver of the second vehicle, and Andy Marquez, who was the commander of the vehicle, both got out. They were severely dazed. I could see Scott Hookey laying on his back about thirty to forty feet away from the vehicle. After a quick personnel check, we realized Doc was missing and still in the vehicle. Toliver and I extinguished the flames enough to where I could open the right rear passenger door where Doc was seated.

When I looked in I could tell that Doc was gone and there was nothing we could do. Our extinguishers were emptied and the flames became intense again. After a quick assessment, Hookey was now first priority. We cut off his pants with trauma shears and I put a pressure dressing on a wound and some other guys put some on him as well. His legs were missing big chunks, and I was concerned that his femoral artery might have been hit. He was bleeding, but not as much as I thought he should from the nature of his wounds. I think the heat from the blast may have cauterized some of his blood vessels and kept him from having a heavy blood flow.

We checked for enemies in houses in the vicinity and there were only families. However, I did notice there were garden hoses in several yards. I connected them together then worked on extinguishing the flames. The fire burned itself out and the water helped put the rest of it out. Unfortunately, Doc never had a chance."

Lance Cpl. Scott Hookey was manning the 50-caliber machine gun on the vehicle when it was struck by the IED. When asked what he remembered, he said:

"Everything went orange and then I remember bouncing off of something. I don't know if it was the vehicle or the ground, but it was probably the ground. Then everything went white. I think I was knocked unconscious for a few seconds. When everything went white I was trying to get air back in my lungs, because the explosion blew the air out of me. At the same time, I was feeling extreme nausea.

The vehicle was blown up in the air and when it came back down to the ground it was on all four tires and facing at about a forty-five-degree angle to the right. I was blown about 20 or 30 feet to the right side of the vehicle. My memory was like snap shots. I don't remember the incident like a movie reel. I remember lying between the third vehicle and the second vehicle. After hearing shots fired my only thought was to seek cover. I remember getting up and wobbling for cover. I couldn't run. I remember seeing the Humvee on fire then I can remember being in front of it, between it and the first vehicle. I just don't remember passing between it and the wall, but that was the only way to get to where I was. I then realized the shots I heard were the 50-Caliber bullets being set off from the burning Humvee. I remember somebody yelling out, 'Where's Sare!?' I remember the convoy commander Cpl. Tobin on the radio asking for assistance. Cpl. Toliver went back toward the Humvee to rescue Sare, but the flames were so intense he could not get close enough to do anything.

While seeking cover, somehow I made it around a corner. This is where the first vehicle stopped. It was while I was around this corner that Cpl. Thomas Katakowski began tending to my wounds. I said to him, 'I think I crapped myself.' Katakowski said, 'That's not crap. It's blood.' I had small slivers of shrapnel in my legs, but the blast ripped pieces of my legs off and now I am actually missing chunks of muscle in my legs, some big enough to put a baseball in. Now my legs always feel fatigued. My legs hurt every day, but I just ignore it."

The IED detonated beneath the vehicle between the right rear tire and the right rear seat where Otter was sitting. He was killed instantly. On October 25, 2006, the Department of Defense posted this "Immediate Release:"

The Department of Defense announced today the death of a sailor who was supporting Operation Iraqi Freedom.

Seaman Charles O. Sare, 23, of Hemet, Calif., died Oct. 23 from enemy action while conducting combat operations in the Al Andar Province, Iraq. Sare, a Hospital Corpsman, was assigned to the Naval Ambulatory Care Center, Port Hueneme, Calif. and was currently serving with the Multi-National Corps – Iraq.

Upon further investigation, it was determined that the IED was made of two anti-tank land minds and one propane tank. Wires running away from the point of detonation suggested that it was manually triggered.

After receiving the news of his son's death, Ed and the notification team proceeded into the house. He called Karen at work. She said:

> "I was at work when he called me, and I screamed and started crying when he told me Otter was killed. Everybody at work asked me what was wrong and when I told them Otter was killed they told me I needed to go immediately."

While Charles waited for Karen he told the three-man notification team they could leave, but they refused to leave him alone. They would not depart until Karen arrived.

Otter was laid to rest on November 2, 2006 at the San Jacinto Valley Cemetery in Hemet, California. His father felt it would be best for his final resting place to be in the town he was born and raised in. Nearly seven hundred grieving friends and relatives attended his funeral. The procession from the church to the cemetery was led by his personal pickup truck and at some intersections cross traffic had to wait more than thirty minutes for the motorcade to pass.

Seven months later, while family and friends were still going through the grieving process, Otter's family was contacted by the military. They had identified subsequent remains through DNA. Otter's family would have to endure a second funeral. Unlike his first funeral, this funeral was very small, very private, and not a big deal was made of it. There was no procession and no large crowd. Because of the short notice, it was restricted to only family members. This time a coffin about the size of a shoebox was placed on top of Otter's original coffin finally putting HN (Hospitalman) Charles Otto Sare to rest. And Otter's father could only sum it up with these words:

"There are no words to describe the hurt."

On October 23, 2011, while standing at Otter's grave site on the fifth anniversary of his passing, Ed said to me,

"The pain doesn't go away."

On March 5, 2016 Ed would lose his battle with cancer. He was laid to rest in the same cemetery as Otter in Hemet, California.

November 2006

Twenty-three days after Otter was laid to rest, on November 25, the San Jacinto Valley would lose their fifth man. Although he lived in Aguanga which is not in the valley itself, it is still part of the Hemet Unified School District.

HN. Charles Otto Sare

This was the last photo taken of Sare approximately two hours before the incident. He is sitting on top of the Humvee he was killed in. The photo was taken by Scott Hookey, the machine gunner of the vehicle.

Lance Cpl. Jeromy David West

Chapter 6
Lance Cpl. Jeromy David West

"I love my job. I love being a marine."
-LCpl. Jeromy D. West

Jeromy was born on September 21, 1986 at St. Joseph's Hospital in Albuquerque, New Mexico. Due to irreconcilable differences, Jeromy's mother and father separated before Jeromy was one year old, and when Jeromy was four he moved to Chula Vista, California, with his mother. At the age of five Jeromy began playing football, and his first coach was Ron Klopf. Ron and Jeromy's mother, Lisa, developed a fondness for each other and began dating. On June 18, 1994, when Jeromy was seven, Ron and Lisa married. In 1995, the family left Chula Vista to settle in Temecula, California.

While eight year old Jeromy and his family were living in Temecula, Jeromy went through a phase where he wanted to protect the dolphins. So, any time his family bought a six-pack of soda he made sure the plastic holder was cut just in case it made its way to the ocean. While he was in this phase Ron took Jeromy fishing and Jeromy caught a trout. Ron took the trout to a cleaning table and pulled out his knife. Jeromy said, "What are you doing?" Ron said, "I'm going to clean the fish." and started cutting. Jeromy thought cleaning the fish meant to wash it off. As Ron began cutting, Jeromy went slightly hysterical saying, "What are you doing?!! What are you doing?!! Awww . . .!!!" There were other people around watching Jeromy's reaction. Ron said, "Jeromy, you don't buy fish in a package like this, you have to clean them out." All the way home, while shaking his head, Jeromy kept saying, "I can't believe you did that."

When Jeromy was eleven -years old Ron took him to a football game in San Diego. The Chargers were playing the 49ers. They were sitting in the end zone. About the fourth row up there was a beach ball bouncing amongst the crowd. Ron said, "Jeromy was just obsessed with that beach ball. He really wanted to get his hands on it." Finally, the beach ball made its way to Jeromy and Ron said, "If you hit it that way it's going to go onto the field and there will be no more beach ball." Jeromy said, "Oh" then turned around to hit it back into the crowd. He hit the ball right into a woman's face, and it bounced out onto the field anyway. Ron said, "You could see the woman was clearly pissed and there was an empty seat next to Jeromy, so I said, 'I'm telling your dad when he gets back.' About 200 people in the crowd were laughing hysterically and some even had beer coming out of their noses."

In 1999, when Jeromy was in the 8th grade, his family settled in the rural area of Aguanga, California, which rests in the San Jacinto mountain range about 18 miles northeast of Temecula. The family was living here when the September 11 attacks occurred. Jeromy told his mother had he been old enough he would have joined the military right then. It was at a very young age that he would frequently tell his mother he wanted to be an "Army Man" just like his grandfather and great-grandfather.

When Jeromy was in high school Ron, Jeromy, Jeromy's brother AJ, and Jeromy's friend Lane stopped at a Cold Stone Creamery in Temecula. While Ron and AJ sat down and conservatively ate their ice cream Jeromy and Lane sat across from each other and said, "One, two, three" and began shoveling spoons full of ice cream in their mouths. After a few moments, they both grabbed their heads and fell on the floor bellowing about the pain in their foreheads. Jeromy said, "I can't see out of my eye!" The two were having a race to see who could get a brain freeze first with astonished spectators watching and wondering. Ron began laughing to the point that ice cream began running out of his nose. When the pain subsided in their heads the two would sit across from each other again and say, "One, two, three, go!" and they started their race to a brain freeze all over again.

Eric Robbins, Jeromy's childhood friend since the age of five, remembered while they were in high school, on most days after school, he and Jeromy would go park in some of the undeveloped cul-de-sacs in their neighborhood and talk. He said, "We would hang out and do the typical teenager things. We would talk about how our day went. We would talk about girls. Sometimes we would steal some of Ron's beer and drink it."

Jeromy's parents' home has a long driveway that climbs a small slope. The top of the driveway levels out at a sharp angle. Eric said:

> "One time we decided to see how much air we could catch off the top of the driveway with a Mercury Tracer. Jeromy would not let me take a turn, so I had to stand at the top and let him know how high off the ground he would get.

After several attempts, he ended up getting about a foot to a foot-and-a-half in the air. After each attempt, he would slam on the brakes. There were a lot of skid marks at the top of the driveway and some bent rebar sticking out of the ground for the new garage that was being built. When Ron came home and saw all the skid marks leading up to the bent rebar he wasn't very happy with us."

Jeromy was an active athlete. He played baseball, football, and wrestled for the Hamilton Bobcats. He told his mother that the football field was his favorite place in the world. Before a game, he just could not wait to go up the steps that led to the field. In fact, he loved playing football so much that he was offered a partial scholarship to play football at Claremont College, but decided he wanted to join the Marines first to save money on the GI Bill then go to college and play football. Ron said:

"I remember his last play in football his senior year was an interception right in front of his grandfather who was standing on the sidelines right next to him. He wanted to go into the Marine Corp on the GI Bill then get out and go play football. That was his plan and he was sticking to it. He wanted to do four years in the Marine Corp then play college ball."

In fact, Jeromy was so adamant about his plan that he brought his mother papers to sign while he was still in high school. She tried to convince him otherwise by taking him to spring football training at College of The Desert in Palm Desert. He thoroughly enjoyed the experience, but he was set on going into the Marine Corp. Lisa knew he would sign the papers himself when he turned 18. Since his graduation was near she signed the papers allowing him to join the Marine Corps infantry at 17. She felt at this point that it was better to support him in what he really wanted to do than to resist.

Jeromy graduated from Hamilton High School in May 2004. He went to the Marine Corps Recruit Depot in San Diego, California for basic training.

He was then sent to Hawaii for six months for advanced training and assigned to the 2nd Battalion, 3rd Marine Regiment, 3rd Marine Division, III Marine Expeditionary Force at Kaneohe Bay, Hawaii.

Jeromy's unit did eight months in Afghanistan from June 2005 until January 2006. Jeromy felt like he was a part of history during this time, because he helped guard voting booths during Afghanistan's elections. After returning from Afghanistan in January 2006, Jeromy spent the next eight months between Hawaii and California. His orders for his second tour of duty came in September 2006. He was ordered to go to Iraq. Before his second deployment he was making sure to spend as much time with family and friends as he possibly could. His mother Lisa said,

> "When he came back from Afghanistan he was different. He was disconnected for a couple of months then the old Jeromy slowly surfaced."

As the old Jeromy slowly resurfaced, Lisa was beginning to get a sense of something she did not want to think about or believe. She said:

> "I never said anything to Jeromy, but I knew he wasn't coming back and I had the sense that he knew that too. He was acting very different. One time he woke me up at one-thirty in the morning and wanted me to go to the casino with him, so I went. He had never done anything like that before. He also spent a lot of time fishing at the lake."

Jeromy was spending an unusual amount of time with friends and family. This was something Ron and Lisa had never seen him do any time prior.

A few weeks before being deployed to Iraq Jeromy and Ron were fishing at the lake in the gated community of Lake Riverside where they lived. Jeromy informed Ron that he had torn his meniscus while training with his men.

He was a mortar man and a very strong kid, so they frequently gave him the heaviest stuff to carry. Jeromy informed Ron that he had a decision to make. He said he could go get surgery on his knee, but that it would be a three-month recovery, so he would miss his deployment to Iraq. Ron said to Jeromy that missing a deployment to Iraq is not such a bad thing. Jeromy said that he decided he was going to go because his captain said he could go and they were going to put him on a Mark-19 Grenade launcher on top of an LAV. Ron said to Jeromy:

"You could do this deployment and it will probably be your last one because by the time you get back you won't have enough time to go on another deployment due to your military time being too short. So, if you miss this deployment there might not be enough time to send you out on another one due to your time being up."

Jeromy replied:,

"No, here's what's going to happen. If I go get my surgery then I will have my three-month recovery and they are going to stick me with a different unit and I do not want to go over there with a bunch of guys I don't know. And I don't want to not go and have somebody killed because I was not there."

Jeromy by-passed his knee surgery, and on September 11, 2006, he was sent to Iraq to begin his second tour of duty, which was to be completed in April of 2007. They were sent to the Al Anbar Province of Iraq. The company he was a part of was the 2/3 Weapons Company, which was made up of about 200 Marines. When they arrived in Iraq they were dispatched to the town of Khan Al Baghdadi, which is northwest of Ramadi. Their assignment was to clear out any insurgents or hostile individuals in the area, then move on to the next small town. They were in Baghdadi approximately three weeks when they were given the order to move north to a small settlement along the Euphrates River named Albu Hayatt approximately 15 to 20 miles southeast of Haditha. While in this new location, according to a good friend of Jeromy's, Cpl. Coleman Elliott, "We were hit once or twice a week by mortars, rockets and IEDs." Another one of Jeromy's comrades, LCpl. Jacob Cook, said:

> "No mortars or rockets ever landed on the house we were occupying, but they did land close by and hit the walls. On one occasion a Lieutenant Colonel took some tiny pieces of shrapnel in the eyes. There was one mortar that set a parked Humvee on fire when it landed in the trunk and an IED just outside our little compound knocked some power lines over that landed on another parked Humvee and caught that one on fire."

On one occasion, according to LCpl. Jacob Cook, Jeromy returned from checkpoint 12, which was approximately four or five miles from the house they occupied. Jeromy proceeded to share how he was sitting at his Mark 19 Grenade Launcher on the Humvee he rode in. Cook said:

> "Jeromy said he was sitting on the seat strap with his feet up smoking a cigarette and just kicking back. This checkpoint was in the middle of nowhere so if anybody was coming toward you, you could see them long before they reached you. Suddenly a mortar hit the ground about 10 yards in front of his vehicle and slightly to the left. Jeromy said he pulled his feet toward himself at the same time he slipped out of the strap and dropped straight into the Humvee as if an invisible hand reached up and pulled him in. His description of the incident was so funny all we could do was laugh. Jeromy was good at getting you to smile or laugh."

About two weeks after they arrived in Albu Hayatt, Jeromy called Ron in early November with what would inevitably be a prophetic statement. Ron was in Las Vegas when he received Jeromy's call. Ron said:

> "I said to Jeromy, 'You gotta be careful of those IEDs.' Jeromy said: 'Nah, I'm not worried about the IEDs, I'm worried about the snipers. Snipers are crazy out here and we don't take any precautions and if I'm going to go it's going to be a sniper. I'm just terrified of these snipers.'"

Jeromy phoned home on Tuesday, November 21 to wish his mother a happy birthday. On Wednesday, November 22, the Humvee Jeromy was riding in was struck by an IED while he was manning the Mark 19 Grenade Launcher. He was ejected and sustained no injuries. However, the next day his back was extremely sore. As a result, he was given Thursday (Thanksgiving Day) and Friday off. He made it a point to call home on Thanksgiving Day, and he spoke to everybody that was at his parent's house. Even after being disconnected several times he called back after each disconnect and made it a point to speak to every relative and every friend that was present.

After his two days off he was assigned to light duty. On Saturday, November 25, 2006, his first light duty assignment was to man a post in one corner of the roof on top of the house they were occupying. There was a weapon in each corner. One corner had a 50. caliber machine gun, another corner had a 240 Gulf Machine gun and the other two corners had Mark 19 Grenade Launchers. Jeromy arrived at about 10:00 a.m. to relieve LCpl. Jacob Cook, the Marine who was manning the Mark 19 in the southwest corner of the roof. They had built a barrier around the house they were occupying and that particular Mark 19 was guarding the entrance to the property. During the shift change, and before Jeromy went to the roof, he pulled out a cigarette and asked Cpl Shaun Duling if he had a light. Cpl. Duling said:

> "Jeromy was heading to his post when he came by and asked if I had a light. I tossed him a white Bic lighter that I still have, then he went upstairs to assume post. I went into the COC (Command Operations Center) to begin radio watch. I am not exactly sure how long I was on watch before it happened, but it could not have been more than twenty or thirty minutes when I heard a 'SNAP!,' like the sound you would hear by snapping a leather belt together that was followed by a loud 'THUD!' After we heard the thud everyone in the COC just froze.

Not a sound was made until a few seconds later when over the radio one of the other posts screamed, "It's West! It's West! He is down!" I began to run out of the COC up to the post when I was grabbed by our Commanding Officer Captain Capuzzi and I remember being told 'I need you in here.' I then started contacting Battalion for a medevac as Doc. De Prisco ran upstairs along with a few other Marines. Our Executive Officer, Lt. Patrick Kinser, ran up there too. He came back down to the COC a few minutes later and the look on his face said it all. He had blood on his uniform and then he said, 'He is gone.' I remember feeling dizzy almost like I had just been punched. Finally, Doc. Deprisco and a few other Marines walked down the stairs carrying the black body bag and I just started crying.

After the initial shock, I went up to the post. There was a lot of blood at the post with some of his gear that had been ripped off and laying there was the lighter I had tossed him. Doc and Lt. Kinser were getting ready to come up and clean up the post, so I grabbed the lighter and headed back down and asked them if they needed any help. They said they would take care of it, so I had to go back on radio watch."

Cpl. Coleman P. Elliot was one of the Marines who just finished his shift. He said:

"I had just finished my eight-hour shift from the Mark 19 that was diagonal to the one Jeromy had gone to. Our operation cycle was eight hours on the roof, eight hours of patrol and eight hours of sleep. I had already walked down the stairs and I was on the first floor in the entryway of where we slept. Usually, we take our armor off, but I still had most of my gear on when somebody yelled, 'Shots fired!' I ran back up the stairs with Cpl. Joseph Thomas. We were there in less than ten seconds. When we made it to the roof I saw Jeromy on his hands and knees near the base of his weapon. I thought he was throwing up, but I realized it was blood coming from his head region. Thomas and I ran over to him, grabbed him and laid him on his back. His whole body went completely relaxed when we laid him back and that was it. He was just not there anymore. He was gone. I helped bring him down the stairs, and I had no idea I had blood all over me until somebody told me to change.

Jeromy and I would talk a lot. He said to me, 'If I die you can have my cigarettes and take this bag to my mom.' He had a plastic bag underneath the armor in his flak jacket. Inside the bag, he had a flag and some small trinkets that friends and family had given him. So, I took it out of his flak jacket and carried it with me for the next four months until I went home. When I was back in the States I was able to hand it to his mother."

Jeromy was struck by a sniper's bullet on his right cheek a few inches below his right temple.

Three men had been terrorizing the area, and a couple days after Jeromy's passing four of Jeromy's fellow Marines decided to go out at 2 a.m. with night vision equipment. From a small structure about a quarter mile from their base camp they watched three Iraqis pull up in a truck and begin to lay down an IED in the middle of a dirt road the Marines used regularly. As the insurgents began their lethal work, the Marines opened fire on them. One of the three dropped immediately. Another one jumped into the vehicle and began to drive off. Unfortunately for him, he drove straight toward the Marines who were shooting at him, and he was shot up in the vehicle as he approached. The third man ran in the opposite direction. One of the Marines said,

"I hit him in the back three times before he made it around a corner of a building. I could tell I hit him, because each time I fired he would twitch really hard so I knew I hit him."

The third individual was found dead along the Euphrates River the next morning. The other two were respectfully laid out in the road near the vehicle so the locals could find them at day break. One of Jeromy's friends said,

"They had parents just like us and they were just fighting for what they believed in just like us so out of respect we just laid them in the road where they could be found the next morning by the locals."

However, a Russian made Kalashnikov sniper rifle was found in their possession. The four-man team felt certain they got the individual who took Jeromy's life.

On November 27, The Department of Defense posted on their "Immediate Release" statement:

The Department of Defense announced today the death of three Marines who were supporting Operation Iraqi Freedom.

Cpl. Nicholas P. Rapavi, 22, of Springfield, Va., died Nov. 24 from wounds sustained while conducting combat operations in Al Anbar province, Iraq. He was assigned to the 2nd Battalion, 8th Marine Regiment, 2nd Marine Division, II Marine Expeditionary Force, Camp Lejeune, N.C.

Cpl. Michael C. Ledsome, 24, of Austin, Texas, died Nov. 25 while conducting combat operations in Al Anbar Province, Iraq. He was assigned to the 3rd Battalion, 2nd Marine Regiment, 2nd Marine Division, II Marine Expeditionary Force, Camp Lejeune, N.C.

Lance Cpl. Jeromy D. West, 20, of Aguanga, Calif., died Nov. 25 while conducting combat operations in Al Anbar Province, Iraq. He was assigned to the 2nd Battalion, 3rd Marine Regiment, 3rd Marine Division, III Marine Expeditionary Force, Kaneohe Bay, Hawaii.

On Saturday, November 25, Jeromy's younger sister, Brandi, was arriving home from Temecula after cheerleading practice. Brandi said:

"I pulled up and there was a van parked in my parking space I thought, 'Who is this?' The van didn't look like a government van.

> It looked like a regular family van, and we always had a lot of people and friends show up at our house, so I didn't think anything of it until I saw them get out of the van. The three of them were wearing their dress blues and I just knew. I was aware that when somebody was killed in a war that they came to your door. The first words they said were, 'I take it you're the sister?' I immediately broke down into tears. I didn't know what to say I just screamed, 'He's gone!' and I just freaked out. I immediately felt sick to my stomach. I remember just wanting to throw up and thinking I was going to pass out. I called my dad on the phone and told him. Afterwards, these guys were trying to hug me and hold me, but I ran into the house and locked myself in the bathroom, because I thought I was going to be sick."

Ron was in San Diego when Brandi called him. He said:

> "My older daughter was moving to Chula Vista, so I got one of Jeromy's football buddies, John, and we went down there to help her move. When I was helping her unload her truck, I got a call from Brandi and she was screaming into the phone saying, 'He's dead, he's dead, he's dead!' I thought she was talking about her dog. She was so hysterical I had no idea what she was talking about and it was hard to understand what she was saying so I said, 'Listen, stop crying and call me when I can understand you,' and I hung up. She called back a few moments later and said, 'Jeromy is dead.' I paused and said, 'Let me get this straight. Just say yes or no to my question. Jeromy is dead?' She said, 'Yes.' I said, 'I'm on my way home.' I had to let Lisa know, but I knew she was driving to a cheer competition with her friend Rhonda at that time and I didn't want to tell her while she was driving so I called Rhonda's phone."

Lisa and Rhonda were on their way to a cheer competition. Lisa was the head coach and her van was filled with all the equipment. They were on the north bound ramp of the 15-Freeway off of Temecula Parkway in Temecula when Rhonda's phone rang. When Rhonda answered, Ron asked where they were. Rhonda said, "We're getting on the freeway."

Ron said, "I need you to pull over right away, because I need to tell her something." Rhonda relayed the message and Lisa responded with, "Tell him we're on the freeway." Ron said, "I want you to have her pull over and then hand her the phone." At this point, Rhonda knew it was something serious. She just did not know what. She relayed the message to Lisa again so when Lisa pulled over at the top of the ramp, Rhonda handed her the phone. When asked what Ron said, Lisa's response was, "I don't even know what he said to me. It's all kind of a blur, but I do remember being kind of pissed off." What Ron said was, "The Marines are at the house and they told Brandi that Jeromy has been killed, so you need to come home."

Rhonda was not sure what Ron said to Lisa. All Rhonda knew is at that moment Lisa went hysterical. Rhonda said,

"Lisa just started saying, 'No, no, no, no' and broke into hysterical crying, then said, 'Jeromy is dead? Are you sure? Are you sure? Is it a mistake? Oh no!' She just lost it. I have never seen her like that. She just went hysterical. There was a lot of disbelief. She said to Ron, 'Maybe they made a mistake. He can't be dead. It can't be true.' She kept thinking that maybe they were going to call her and say it wasn't true."

They drove back to Rhonda's house and had a friend take the van with the equipment to the competition. Rhonda then drove Lisa home. Rhonda said:

"Lisa cried all the way home and I started crying. I just didn't know what to do. Lisa kept saying how bad she felt for Brandi having to be there all alone when she found out."

Lisa called her friend Shelley and told her what happened and told her that Brandi was alone. When Rhonda and Lisa arrived about an hour later there was a house full of people already there.

Jeromy's mother Lisa said:

"When they brought Jeromy home, on December 1, (2006) they took us to the San Diego airport. We watched his plane land, then they took us outside and we drove around to the tarmac. When we got out of the car they had already unloaded his casket, and it was sitting at the bottom of the cargo door. I wasn't sure what to expect, but when I came around the car instead of grief being my first emotion I had this overwhelming sense of pride overtake me. It was almost as if this sense of pride is what Jeromy felt, and then five seconds later I felt the grief set in. Jeromy had an escort Marine travel with him from Iraq and all the passengers stayed on the plane until this Marine was let off and Jeromy was unloaded. After Jeromy was unloaded we looked up at the terminal windows near the boarding gate and it was packed with passengers watching the ceremony. There were faces plastered along the windows for as far as I could see. The tarmac was suddenly packed with people. Everybody that worked there was on the tarmac and all the motorcycle policemen that escorted us down there were also on the tarmac. This was one o'clock in the morning and there were people everywhere."

Before Jeromy left for his first tour of duty, Lisa said:

"I told him that if something happened that I wanted him to go to a national cemetery like his grandfather, but he did not want that."

At first, he avoided the conversation by not saying anything, but eventually he said he wanted his body cremated. He wanted a simple ceremony at his most favorite place in the world, the Hamilton High School football field then he asked that Ron and Lisa keep his ashes at home with them.

On the cold evening of December 4, 2006, nearly one thousand people filled the stands at the Hamilton High football field for Jeromy's memorial service. Jeromy's stepbrother A.J., who was serving in the Navy at the time, carried Jeromy's cremated remains out of the team room and up the steps that lead to the field.

This was the same path Jeromy traveled before each home game. Lisa said, "He always said he just couldn't wait to go up those steps, so we took him back to the place that he loved." Also, in honor of Jeromy's wishes Ron and Lisa keep Jeromy's ashes at home in a custom oak box topped with a sculpture.

Jeromy's mother said:

"I think the one thing is that we don't like to focus on how he died. We focus on how he lived, but when you go from a Blue Star family to a Gold Star family it affects your soul. It changes you. It changes how you look at everything. It changes how you view your work. It changes how you view your friends. It changes how you view your life. It changes how you view other people's behavior. It changes how you view everything that you thought was important to you. It really changes you.

We don't have that fun, wild, prankster Jeromy anymore and we miss that. We are all still together as a family, but Jeromy was an important link to all of us. He was special. There was just something about that kid that was special and we don't have that. We get to sit around and tell the stories about it, but we don't get to live it anymore."

Ron said:

"I was with a friend who was getting a little irritated with his son who was a little late for an event. When the guy started to express his displeasure, I said, 'It's okay, at least he's alive.' That seemed to help the guy calm down and stop making a big deal out of something that was not that big of a deal. It might have been a big deal to him, but it was trivial to me.

We don't get to see this great kid and what he could have been. It stops here. It just stops. I would love to have seen him now, older, maybe with kids."

Jeromy's mother added:

> "He would have been a great dad. He loved being an uncle. We see his friends now and they all have kids. I wonder where he would have been. Would he still be with Nancy who he said was the love of his life? I wonder. I wish we knew. It's the little things that I'm going to miss the most. Like him kissing me on my cheek. I am going to miss him every day for the rest of my life."

Jeromy's sister Brandi said,

> "We continue to carry the burden and people forget. Even our close friends have moved on while we continue to suffer."

February 2, 2006

Less than two months after Jeromy was laid to rest the Hemet and San Jacinto Valley would receive word of their sixth fatality, Chief Warrant Officer Keith Yoakum.

True Cost of Liberty - The Burden of Freedom

Lance Cpl. Jeromy David West

CW4. Keith Yoakum

Chapter 7
CW4. Keith Yoakum

Keith was born in Hemet, California on November 24, 1965 to his mother Phoebe Yoakum and father G. A. Yoakum. Keith was born eight minutes ahead of his twin brother Kevin. He was also the sibling to the oldest child, Mark, who was ten years older, his older sister Maryann who was seven years older, and an older brother Eric who was born June 10, 1964. Eric passed away at seven months old. Keith and Kevin never had the chance to meet Eric.

His father G. A. Yoakum said, "When he was a kid, if Keith drew a picture of a horse, a rabbit, or a heart for Valentine's Day, somewhere in the picture you would find an airplane or helicopter." He dreamed of flying as a small child, and after he graduated from Hemet High School in 1984, he saved enough money from odd jobs for flying lessons and soloed in a single engine plane at the age of nineteen. Shortly thereafter he earned his private pilot's license.

While he worked to save flying money, Keith attended Mount San Jacinto Community College in San Jacinto, California for two years and earned his Associates degree. It was in college where he met Kelly Conklin, his wife-to-be and they would have two daughters, Katelynn and Kirstee. Eventually, the family would settle in Alabama on a piece of property with enough acreage to build a landing strip. Keith wanted his own runway to fly his plane from once he retired from the military.

Keith enlisted in the United States Army in September 1986 and served as a light wheel vehicle mechanic at Fort Campbell, Kentucky. After completing Initial Entry Rotary Wing Aeroscout Course at Fort Rucker, Alabama in February 1992, he was assigned to the 5th Battalion, 501st Aviation Regiment at Camp Eagle, Korea. Keith completed the AH-64A Aircraft Qualification Course at Fort Rucker, Alabama in August 1993. In August of 1998, he was deployed to Bosnia in support of Operation Joint Forge. In 1999, he was sent to Albania as part of Operation Allied Force and Kosovo as a part of Operation Joint Guardian.

While he was in the Army, he earned his Bachelor degree in Professional Aeronautics from Embry-Riddle Aeronautical University. He had been asked to work for the FAA and planned on either working for the FAA or flying forestry fire fighting air tankers upon retiring from the Army.

Yoakum was selected to fly for the United States Parachute Team, the `Golden Knights,` in November 2005 at Fort Bragg, North Carolina, but he turned down the opportunity and elected to return to the AH-64D Longbow Apache and deploy to Iraq.

In 2006, Keith was stationed in South Korea flying fixed wing aircraft for military intelligence along the 38th parallel. Near the end of this tour he phoned his parents to inform them that he would be volunteering for a tour in Iraq. Keith's mother Ann said:

> "When he called, and told us he was doing a tour in Iraq, I said, 'Keith, please don't go.' And he said, 'Mom, it's something I have to do.' I knew then that he was not going to come back. He was going to go back to Alabama for leave before going to Texas and then Iraq, so I said to his dad, 'We're going to go back to see him,' because I just knew then that he was not going to come back. So, we had a little Honda Hybrid and we made room in the back for the dog and drove out there. We spent a few days with him, because I knew he wasn't going to make it. I knew he was not going to come back. It was a feeling and I just knew."

In July 2006, he was assigned to 1st Battalion, 227th Aviation Regiment at Fort Hood, Texas where he served as an AH-64D Maintenance Test Pilot. He deployed to Iraq in support of Operation Iraqi Freedom in September 2006.

On the morning of February 2, 2007, two AH-64D Longbow Apache helicopters departed from their base in Taji, Iraq, about 12 miles north of Baghdad, on a reconnaissance mission in order to support four ground brigades. Keith was piloting the second aircraft, the trailing helicopter. As they flew over a section of Taji they began to receive machine gun and anti-aircraft fire from a well-established ambush with intertwining fields of enemy gun fire. A heavy barrage of tracers and machine gun bullets coming from multiple directions overtook the Apaches and immediately riddled the fuselage of Keith's helicopter.

After the two helicopters escaped the deadly enemy kill zone, Keith announced on his radio that he "lost utility hydraulics." This is a serious situation that requires the pilot to land immediately if there is a safe place to land. The two helicopters headed out of the kill zone and assessed their situation. The loss of hydraulic pressure put Keith's main gun out of commission, but he still had use of his 2.75 inch rockets. However, it would require him to aim the helicopter at the targets he wished to strike. Keith radioed one more time, "We've got no utility hydraulics left." Even though he was in a critical situation, he refused to leave his wingman and radioed to his wingman, "I can put rockets in."

Keith did not want this enemy left to come back and strike again. Keith's instructions to the lead helicopter were, "you find them, we've got you covered." About two minutes later the two aircrafts headed back into the kill zone in hopes of putting the anti-aircraft guns and their crews out of commission. While losing critical hydraulic pressure, Keith said, "I'm going to climb up and cover you from high and we're gonna work on rockets." His damaged aircraft only afforded him the chance to go up high and dive toward the enemy in order to provide effective rocket fire, while eliminating collateral damage to surrounding homes. A few moments after his last radio call, as they were in-bound to the kill zone, the lead helicopter radioed to Keith Yoakum's helicopter, and there was no response.

After several more transmissions with no response the lead Apache turned around and spotted the smoke from the burning wreckage where Keith's helicopter crashed. Chief Warrant Officer Keith Yoakum and his copilot, Chief Warrant Officer Jason Garth Defrenn, 34, of Barnwell, S.C, were both killed instantly.

The Department of Defense posted in their immediate report:

The Department of Defense announced today the death of two soldiers who were supporting Operation Iraqi Freedom. They died Feb. 2 in Taji, Iraq, of wounds suffered when their Apache helicopter was forced to land during combat operations. Both soldiers were assigned to the 1st Battalion, 227th Aviation Cavalry Regiment, 1st Cavalry Division, Fort Hood, Texas. Killed were:

Chief Warrant Officer Jason G. Defrenn, 34, of Barnwell, S.C.

Chief Warrant Officer Keith Yoakum, 41, of Hemet, Calif.

The incident is under investigation.

For his bravery, Keith Yoakum was posthumously awarded the Distinguished Service Cross. He was the eighth soldier since Vietnam to earn the award and the first Army aviator since Vietnam to be awarded the Distinguished Service Cross. It is the military's second-highest medal of valor only second to the Medal of Honor. On November 11, 2007, his wife, children, siblings, and parents received this award on his behalf at a ceremony on Veterans Day at Gibbel Park in Hemet, Calif. His widow Kelly and his parents each received their own medal.

In addition to his Distinguished Service Cross, Keith also earned:

The Bronze Star
The Purple Heart
Meritorious Service Medal with two Oak Leaf Clusters
The Air Medal
The Army Commendation Medal with five Oak Leaf Clusters
The Army Achievement Medal with 2 Oak Leaf Clusters
The Army Good Conduct Medal
The National Defense Service Medal with one Bronze Star
The Armed Forces Expeditionary Medal
The Kosovo Campaign Medal with Bronze Star
The Iraqi Campaign Medal
The Global War on Terrorism Medal
The Korean Defense Service Medal
The Non-Commissioned Officer Professional Development Ribbon The Army Service Ribbon
The Overseas Service Ribbon with Bronze Numeral 4
The NATO Medal
The Combat Action Badge
The Air Assault Badge
The Parachutist Badge
The Master Army Aviator Badge

His foreign country awards include:

Egyptian Aviator Wings
German Aviator Wings
The German Armed Forces Proficiency Badge

CW4. Keith Yoakum

**On May 4, 2009, Keith was inducted into
the Army Aviation Hall of Fame**

February 7, 2006

Five days after Keith Yoakum's helicopter went down the Hemet and San Jacinto Valley would receive word of their seventh fatality Sgt. Travis Dwight Pfister. Like Keith Yoakum, Travis would also lose his life in a helicopter incident along with six other comrades.

Sgt. Travis Dwight Pfister

Chapter 8
Sgt. Travis Dwight Pfister

Al-Karmah, Iraq
February 7, 2007

They flew toward the enemy in a CH – 46 Sea Knight Helicopter unsuspecting of what was about to happen. It is a military machine; however, not so much a killing machine. A CASEVAC is a unit that flies helicopters into hostile enemy territory to remove combat injured personnel while providing critical emergency care. Essentially, CASEVAC is a transport and a military ambulance, but the insurgents only saw an opportunity to strike back at the supporters of Israel, the *"Great Satan,"* the United States. With a camera in hand, the enemy waited to assault the helicopter approaching them.

Whether they knew it was a crime against humanity to shoot down a CASEVAC aircraft or not their objective was unimpeded, and their intentions were malevolent. For unknown reasons Capt. Jennifer J. Harris made a right turn. At about the 180-degree point of her turn smoke can be seen from the area of the camera filming the incident, the type of smoke that comes from the back of a small missile fired from a shoulder launched assault weapon. Then there was an impact at the back of the helicopter. The Sea Knight continued to fly for about a minute before becoming engulfed in flames and making a crash landing killing all onboard.

This was five days after Keith Yoakum was killed in his helicopter crash. Crew Chief Sgt. Travis Dwight Pfister was on board and he would become the seventh Hemet resident to make the ultimate sacrifice.

Born July 22, 1979 in Pasco, Washington, Travis lived with his Marine Corp. sergeant wife Jessica in Hemet, California, and according to an article written for *"Fallen Heroes Project"* the two met at a party at Camp Pendleton where Travis was stationed. They had been married for five and a half years. Travis was a Helicopter Crew Chief with the HMM-364 Purple Foxes for eight and a half years and was due home from his third tour in Iraq the following month. According to Iraqiwarheroes.org:

> "In an e-mail to his mom last week, Pfister wrote that he'd taken more than 20 people to the hospital for urgent medical care this month alone." He also wrote, "Things are going well, though just waiting to come home. I love you guys and will see you all soon."

The video of the shoot down was shown on numerous news stations due to the fact that seven personnel lost their lives. It was a tragedy to seven American families and a harsh reminder how expensive freedom is.

In their Immediate Release announcement, the Department of Defense posted:

The Department of Defense announced today the death of five Marines who were supporting Operation Iraqi Freedom.

> *Capt. Jennifer J. Harris, 28, of Swampscott, Mass.*
> *1st Lt. Jared M. Landaker, 25, of Big Bear City, Calif.*
> *Sgt. Travis D. Pfister, 27, of Richland, Wash.*
> *Cpl. Thomas E. Saba, 30, of Toms River, N.J.*
> *Sgt. James R. Tijerina, 26, of Beasley, Texas*

All five Marines died Feb. 7 when the helicopter they were flying in crashed while supporting combat operations in Al Anbar Province, Iraq.

Harris, Landaker, Pfister, and Tijerina were assigned to Marine Medium Helicopter Squadron 364, Marine Aircraft Group 39, 3rd Marine Aircraft Wing, I Marine Expeditionary Force, Camp Pendleton, Calif.

Saba was assigned to Marine Medium Helicopter Squadron 262, Marine Aircraft Group 36, 1st Marine Aircraft Wing, III Marine Expeditionary Force, Okinawa, Japan.

The cause of the incident is under investigation.

In a separate release the Department of Defense posted:

The Department of Defense announced today the death of two sailors who were supporting Operation Iraqi Freedom.

Petty Officer 1st Class Gilbert Minjares Jr., 31, of El Paso, Texas, and Petty Officer 3rd Class Manuel A. Ruiz, 21, of Federalsburg, Md., died Feb. 7 in a helicopter crash in Al Anbar Province, Iraq.

The cause of the crash is under investigation.

Minjares was assigned to Marine Aircraft Group 14, 2nd Marine Aircraft Wing, Cherry Point, N.C., and Ruiz was assigned to 2nd Medical Battalion, 2nd Marine Logistics Group, II Marine Expeditionary Force, Camp Lejeune, N.C.

The foundation's mission statement reads:

"To make a positive impact on the children of both Wounded and Fallen military personnel through financial, emotional, and educational assistance."

The online "Seven Stars Foundation" has been created in their memory, which can be reached at :

www.sevenstarsfoundation.com

March 7, 2007

Exactly one month after Travis Pfister gave the ultimate sacrifice, the town of Hemet would hear of their eighth loss, SSG. Christopher Ralph Webb.

Staff Sgt. Christopher Ralph Webb

Chapter 9
Staff Sgt. Christopher Ralph Webb

Chris was deployed to Iraq on October 30, 2006, two hours ahead of his younger brother Coy. The two brothers were in the same unit and would meet up again in Kuwait. They spent a week together before Chris was sent to Camp Liberty, Iraq and Coy was sent to Taji. The two camps were about fifteen minutes apart.

On the morning of March 7, 2007, Coy was just finishing with a night shift. He said:

"That night I had worked a late shift. When I was done, I went to chow then I went to my bunk. My brother was online just before he was getting ready to head out, so I got to talk to him. I just told him how things were with me and we caught up on things with each other then he said he had to go out on a mission. I said to him that I just got off work and that I would catch him later on tonight. I went to sleep and about two hours after I was asleep there was a pounding on my door. I opened the door and it was my NCO who said, 'You need to come up and have a talk with us.' At that moment, I knew something was up and I kind of figured it was my grandmother back home, because she wasn't doing very well. As we were walking along, my NCO was in front of me and would not let me get next to him. He just stayed in front of me. As soon as we walked into his office I could see the Chaplin, my CO, and others. Right then I knew there was a loss. It still wasn't registering that it could have been my brother. I was still thinking it was somebody back home. They sat me down. They took my rifle from me, and all I heard was the date, the time, and your brother Staff Sergeant Webb. They said, 'On March 7th at 12:30 p.m. your brother Staff Sergeant Christopher Webb was on a convoy and was struck by an IED.' From that point on I don't remember anything else. I just sat there numb and in shock taking it all in. I found out about thirty minutes after it happened, and they told me I could not call home because I had to wait until the rest of the family was notified. They said that as soon as they found out that the rest of the family was notified they would tell me so I could call home. I sat around for about twelve hours waiting for them to inform me that the rest of the family had been notified."

Chris was born on December 16, 1978 in Hemet, California at Hemet Hospital to parents Teresa Hoffmann and Robert Lee Webb Jr. Shortly after Chris's birth his mother joined the Army and was stationed in Tacoma, Washington. While in Tacoma the Webb family had their second child, Susan, on April 23, 1981.

While growing up Chris and his sister were close and when Chris was not playing with his friends he and Susan did nearly everything together. Chris never liked seeing his sister upset so any time she was sad he would put a smile back on her face by singing "Chantilly Lace." She said:

> "One day when I was feeling sad on a drive back to California from Arizona, Chris sang Chantilly Lace as loud as he could for several hours nearly non-stop. He actually sang it until he lost his voice and could not sing or talk for the rest of the day, but every time he saw me get sad he would start singing and I would start smiling."

At the age of six when Chris was in the first grade his parents divorced, and Chris began to act out in school. When his mother would leave for work after dropping him off he would walk back to their apartment and sit at home all day. His mother found out when the upstairs neighbor informed her that she could hear noise downstairs during the day. From that point on Chris never really seemed to like school. His mother said, "Chris was always very intelligent and looking back I now realize he could have been bored because it was too easy for him." It was difficult to get Chris to sit down and do his homework. However, he began playing the saxophone and enjoyed it. His only complaint was that he had to carry it home from school and it was heavy.

According to his mother Chris was very military oriented from a young age and was a "hands-on" individual. He was much more interested in doing things rather than learning from a book. He enjoyed building models, mainly military models. He enjoyed the Civil Air Patrol and when they lived in Winchester, California, (Part of the Hemet Unified School District) he and his childhood friend from kindergarten, Josh Epstein, would play in the hilly rocky land of the area digging fox holes, making military type forts, and playing army together on a regular basis. This was something Chris loved doing and never seemed to get tired of.

Chris and Josh joined the football team their freshman year at West Valley High School. In tenth grade Josh continued with football, but Chris did not. His dislike for public education continued, and he was caught ditching for nine weeks his sophomore year. As a result, he was given the option to finish his education through the Adult Education Program Independent Studies. He chose Adult Education. While in the program Chris decided he wanted to join the military. However, his father Robert did not want him to. He was completely against it. On the other hand, his mother, who came from a strong military background, thought it would be honorable for her son to join the military and serve his country. So, when Chris was seventeen his mother gave her consent for Chris to join the National Guard.

He went to the National Guard's basic training camp from May to August of 1996 and attended One Station Unit Training at Fort Knox, Kentucky. When he completed the training, he came back home and continued on with his Adult Education in order to earn his diploma. At the same time, he was obligated to one weekend a month with the National Guard at their Facility in Banning, California. While he was there they taught him how to drive a tank which was something he enjoyed thoroughly. His experience driving tanks made it clear to him that he belonged in the Army, so when he was eighteen he earned his GED then signed for himself to transfer to the Army on November 14, 1997. Once in the Army he was sent to Fort Sill, Oklahoma for his Advanced Individual Training (AIT). When this was completed he was sent to Camp Casey, South Korea from 1998 to 1999. Upon returning from Korea, he was stationed at Fort Lewis, Washington from 1999 to 2003.

In the year 2000, he met Shalan Harris in Tacoma, Washington at Jillian's Bar and Restaurant. On June 30, 2001, they were married. In 2003, he was assigned to a three-year recruiting duty in Red Bank, New Jersey.

For three years in a row he was named the Top Recruiter for the Mid-Atlantic Battalion. As a result, he earned the Gold Recruiter Badge and three sapphires. At the end of his three-year recruiter's duty he was sent to Fort Hood, Texas.

On September 2, 2006, Chris and Shalan became the proud parents of Mary Verana Webb. Chris only had a short time to spend with his daughter, because two months later, on October 30, he and his brother Coy were both deployed to Iraq. Originally the Army wanted Chris to remain in the States and continue to recruit, but according to Chris's mother he wanted something else. She said:

> "He kept telling me that he wanted to go over there because he was putting soldiers in and he knew a lot of them were ending up over in Iraq. He had a lot of guilt over that."

Chris did not want to send soldiers to a place where he would not go himself.

Upon Chris's departure Shalan decided to leave Fort Hood and go stay with her parents in Alturas, California. She felt more comfortable staying with her immediate family and raising Mary while Chris was deployed.

On the evening of March 7, Shalan and her family returned home from an awards ceremony at her younger brother's high school in Alturas, California. They had been home about twenty minutes when there was a knock at the door. Shalan said:

> "My brother was a senior in high school and his friends were always coming and going, so when I heard the knock I thought it was his friends and I said out loud, 'Can somebody get that?' When there was no response, I said, 'I guess I'll get it myself since I have to do everything else around here.' I was being the overly dramatic older sister at that moment, because I had a baby. So, I picked up the baby and went to the door. When I made it there I could see through the windows that ran along each side of the door two highway patrol men and a military guy. I immediately said, 'I'm not getting it! I'm not getting it!'

> I stepped away from the door. I didn't want to open it. I think it was my brother who finally opened it. I don't remember much after that, but I do remember the soldier asking me if I was Shalan Webb. I remember saying, 'Please not here. Please no! Please no!' He said, 'Ma'am, I have to say it.' Then he said, 'We regret to inform you that your husband Chris has been killed in the line of duty.' It felt like my heart fell to the floor.
> After the initial shock, nearly an hour later I was debating on calling Teresa and letting her know. I asked the soldier that was there if she was going to be notified, and he had to call his CO to see if they were going to let her know. A little while later he said that they would be contacting her first thing in the morning. I remember thinking if the roles were reversed I would have wanted her to call me and let me know. I would not have wanted to go a whole night without knowing."

On that same evening, his mother's phone rang. It was Shalon on the other end. Teresa said

> "I was at home. It was about 9 in the evening. It was an unspoken rule that Shalon and I didn't call each other after 8 p.m., because Mary was asleep so I knew it had to be something important. She was crying and said something about Chris and I knew by the way she sounded it wasn't good, so I kept trying to get more out of her and she couldn't speak. She said that they would be coming to see me in the morning and finally she said, 'He was killed by an IED.' I started screaming hysterically, threw the phone to the floor. My husband held me down in the chair and my daughter Susan picked it up from there."

Susan said,

> "When I heard my mom scream, I knew my brother was killed, but I needed to hear Shalon say it. I had to take the phone around the corner so I could hear it. I had to hear her say it to me before I could completely believe it. It was devastating. I could feel my mind trying to fool me into pretending he was not gone. I think it was the only way my mind could cope with it at that time."

The military bereavement team arrived early the next morning.

Teresa said:

"They were there right at 6 a.m. My husband and I stayed up all night and I was sitting on the porch waiting for them. Two of them showed up in a white military van. Now I have a hard time when I see a white military van."

On March 7, 2007, a three-vehicle convoy was assembled and ordered to depart Camp Liberty, Iraq. According to military reports their mission was to drive to Baghdad International Airport and pick up some dignitaries in order to safely return them to Camp Liberty. Upon arrival, the dignitaries were not present. The convoy was then issued an order to clear a particular route that was known for having IEDs. They stopped and cleared a previous IED site then continued northbound. They were heading north on a worn-out asphalt road that paralleled a canal off to their right. At approximately 12:30 p.m., the convoy turned right in order to cross over the canal on a narrow temporary bridge that was filled with dirt. As the lead vehicle came off the bridge on the other side of the canal it was struck by an IED. Chris was killed instantly. Also killed instantly with Chris was:

Spc. Shawn P. Rankinen, 28, of Independence, Missouri.
Spc. Michael D. Rivera, 22, from Brooklyn, New York

Spc. Michael D. Rivera was bleeding from severe neck wounds. He would die later in the Medevac helicopter on the way to the hospital.

According to a military report:

> "We continued . . . at a very slow and deliberate pace . . . SSG Webb would stop occasionally to inspect suspicious areas and we would dismount when necessary. At about 12:30 we passed (an) intersection . . . and the lead vehicle was struck by an IED. This is where the route passes over a canal and creates a choke point. The lead vehicle had been about 50 – 75 meters in front of our vehicle and I saw it lift up initially in the explosion, but the vehicle was obscured by the flame and dust. My driver came to a stop and I called the Diablo CP with an initial IED contact report. By this time the initial explosion had dissipated and we could see the vehicle laying on its roof on the left side of the road. . . ."

There were four Soldiers in the lead Humvee when it was struck. Spc. Rodolpho Ramirez, who was 21 at the time, was the driver and the only survivor. When asked about his account of the incident, he said:

> "We were instructed to clear a particular route that had not been cleared in a while. A week earlier three soldiers and an Iraqi interpreter were killed on this route by an IED. Our Captain in the second vehicle thought that we should clear it. I remember thinking we should not be here in Humvees. I saw the crater from the last IED that killed the three soldiers and their interpreter a week earlier. I was thinking about them as I slowly snaked my way down the road around areas that I thought could be IED spots. I did not envision we would be hit ten minutes later. It was a blacktop road and they would cut pieces of the blacktop out to put IEDs in then they would put the piece of blacktop back in place. I was snaking my way around areas that looked like IED spots. At one spot I went to the left instead of the right when it hit us. I remember I was staring down the road and everything went black. When everything was black I remember thinking 'Is this dying? Am I dying?'

I remember moaning and I couldn't breathe because my body armor was pressed against my throat as my helmet pushed my chin down toward my chest. The next thing I remember was staring up at the sky wondering what the hell happened as there were guys looking down at me. I was trying to get up as soon as my eyes opened and they kept saying, "Stay down, stay down." They were asking me what my Social Security number was. I thought I was okay, but then I looked at my left elbow and it had been damaged from the explosion. I also felt some blood trickling down my face. I received a small piece of shrapnel in my scalp just below my helmet, but that was it for me. I didn't know the severity of the damage until they helped me up and I staggered back to the second Humvee in the convoy. I looked back at my Humvee and saw that it was upside down and pretty much ripped in half.

I feel guilty a lot now for being the only survivor. I keep thinking that I could have done something to avoid it. I guess I have to thank the radio that was to my right. It shielded me from the blast.

Staff Sergeant Webb has never left my side. When I would get down on myself I would think of what Sergeant Webb would say to me, and I couldn't let myself get discouraged. I was a nervous wreck when I first got to Iraq. Driving a big Humvee around in an area that was full of IEDs was a difficult place for me to drive around in, but Sergeant Webb never gave up on me. He never let me give up, never let me get discouraged, and he never gave up on me. I became his fulltime driver.

The other guys were also motivated and dedicated guys. Rivera had a baby girl. They left so much with me in the little time I got to know them. War is hell, but it is also the best brotherhood there is when you fought with the guys you fought with."

When asked about the official report stating that they were supposed to pick up dignitaries at the airport Spc. Ramirez said, "No, I never heard anything about that. We just had an officer who decided that we should go clear IEDs on a road that was known for having them and Sergeant Webb would never disagree or question. He would just follow orders."

On March 9, 2007, in their "Immediate Release" statement, the Department of Defense wrote:

The Department of Defense announced today the death of three soldiers who were supporting Operation Iraqi Freedom. They died Mar. 7 in Baghdad, Iraq, when an improvised explosive device detonated near their vehicle during combat operations. They were assigned to the 2nd Battalion, 5th Cavalry Regiment, 1st Brigade, 1st Cavalry Division, Fort Hood, Texas.

Killed were:

Staff Sgt. Christopher R. Webb, 28, of Winchester, Calif.
Spc. Shawn P. Rankinen, 28, of Independence, Mo.
Spc. Michael D. Rivera, 22, of Brooklyn, N.Y.

Chris was buried in Alturas, California on March 17, 2007 where his wife and daughter lived. Chris's remains were flown into a small airport in Lakeview, Oregon. From there the procession drove the 54 miles south to Alturas, California. Word got out that a fallen hero would be heading down the 395 Highway, so employees from every government building came out to the street waving flags and saluting the procession as it passed by. Firemen, police officers, Highway Patrol, state and city workers as well as countless civilians paid their respects. It did not take the family's pain away, but there was an element of comfort in the respect that complete strangers displayed towards Chris' sacrifice. Chris' sister Susan said:

"For siblings, it is different. Parents are acknowledged, but siblings at the time of Chris's death were not paid for to go to the funerals. I think they have changed it since then, but siblings have a strong bond too. Chris and I had a strong bond, but they did not acknowledge us siblings like they acknowledged my parents."

About three months after Chris's death the stress of the situation created a baffling situation for Teresa. She said:

"I left work to go home. I had lived in the valley 40 years at that time and I knew the area very well, but that day I decided to take a different side road and for some reason it disoriented me. Even when I made it back onto the street I normally took I couldn't figure out where I was."

Teresa ended up going in the complete opposite direction without knowing it. It then occurred to her that she should call her brother. Only after telling him the names of the streets as she passed by them was he able to direct her home.

"The next thing I was able to recognize was my front gate when I finally made it home. I was unable to recognize a single thing until I made it to my house."

Chris's sister Susan was also struggling. She said:

"For three and a half months after Chris's death I had very little sleep and I lost forty pounds within the first year. While I was going through this I remembered something Chris told me one time when I was having a bad day. He said, 'Susan, there are thousands of people going through what you are going through right now. You're not alone.' At that time, I remember being mad at him for saying that to me, but it actually did help me get through some of the tough times I went through after losing him."

On Teresa's birthday, July 11, 2007, Shalon called her to tell her that she had some news about Chris, but that she did not want this news to ruin her birthday. Teresa said, "I told her that she had to tell me now, or I would stay up all night worrying about it." Shalon started crying and eventually said they had identified some more of Chris's remains. The two talked about it and decided to have his subsequent remains taken to Alturas with his primary remains. For a moment they entertained the thought of having his subsequent remains sent to southern California so both sides of the family would have a place to visit.

However, not wanting to confuse Chris's daughter Mary, they decided to keep his second set of remains in Alturas. Teresa asked Shalon if she would be okay with Coy escorting this set of remains to Alturas. Shalon liked that idea.

Teresa said:

"At the time, they said the IED that killed Chris was a much bigger one than what they usually experienced, one of the biggest ones they had seen."

Chris's sister Susan added:

"When they tell you that they identified your brother by his uniform and through the process of elimination you know he did not feel anything or know anything. He went quickly."

Chris's brother Coy was flown to Dover, Delaware, but before he could be an escort he had to go through a two-day class on how to properly handle the casket. When he completed the class Coy and his brother's remains were flown once again to Lakeview Airport in Oregon. A big deal was not made about Chris's second funeral. Teresa said:

"We didn't have quite as many people there, but because it was such a small community Shalon's family requested a hearse and a highway patrol car to lead it."

Chris's subsequent remains were delivered in a baby-sized casket. It was placed on top of his primary casket then both were covered for the last time.

Like any family who has lost a loved one Chris's family has been challenged by his sudden departure. His mother Teresa said:

"The pain never goes away. You just learn to live with it. Sometimes it just hits you. There are many days in a row when everything is fine then some days there is pain and tears that just seem to come out of the blue. It never really goes away. It changes from day to day. I don't ever want any of our fallen heroes to be forgotten, especially my son.

On the other hand, sometimes the thoughts are so consuming that I tell myself, 'This has to stop and I have to focus on something else,' but at the same time I don't ever want my son to be forgotten, so what are you going to do?"

Chris's sister said:

"He was the one stable man in my life. I would call him for advice. It is an incredible burden that he was killed in action and that he is never coming back and I will never see him again. I went through a phase where I felt angry at Chris for choosing to go to Iraq. The family dynamic has really changed since his death. I have learned that little choices can end up having big consequences."

Chris's widow Shalon said:

"When you're told of something like this it's like you have been kicked in the stomach and you can't catch your breath and it goes on for days. Then you don't even realize it's going away. It does let up some, but it is overwhelming when it happens.

Part of me died that day and within the first 24 hours of being notified of his death anytime my phone rang I knew it was going to be Chris telling me he was okay, and it was a big mistake. I had to wait a year for him not to come home before I could get some closure.

It has been heartbreaking to watch my daughter grow up without a dad especially when she sees all the other kids with their fathers. When she was four, and after we moved to New Jersey, she would say, 'Are the guys that killed my daddy going to get me too?' She used to have nightmares about it. 'When I grow up I'm going to Iraq and I'm going to get the guys who did this to my dad.'

I will never stop loving him and that has made it difficult for me to move on. I do want to get married and have a family someday. I just hope when the right guy comes along, I don't feel guilty or shrink away from him, because he isn't Chris. Even six years later it still comes as a shock to me when I start to think, 'How could he be dead? How could my healthy strong husband be dead? And why am I still crying about this?'"

In his military experience, Chris earned:

The Army Commendation Medal
The Army Achievement Medal
The Army Good Conduct Medal four times
The National Defense Service Medal
The Global War on Terrorism Medal
The Korea Defense Service Medal
The Army Service Ribbon
The Bronze Star
The Purple Heart
The Combat Action Badge

Staff Sgt. Christopher Ralph Webb

Spc. Agustin Gutierrez

March 29, 2007

Three weeks after the death of SSG Webb, the Hemet and San Jacinto Valley would experience their ninth loss: 19-year-old Army Spc. Agustin Gutierrez, born June 9, 1987. He would pass away on March 29, 2007 due to injuries sustained in a non-combat related vehicle accident that occurred on March 28th while traveling with a military convoy in Northern Kabul, Afghanistan. He was born in Escondido, California and graduated from San Jacinto High School in 2005. Sgt. Edmund Wayne McDonald, 25, of Casco, Maine was also killed in the accident. He too would pass away on March 29th due to injuries sustained the day before.

Staff Sgt. Bryan Eugene Bolander

Chapter 10
Staff Sgt. Bryan Eugene Bolander

"The Plague" that hit the Valley would rear its ugly head thirteen months to the day that Army Spc. Agustin Gutierrez was killed. Army Staff Sgt. Bryan Eugene Bolander would be the tenth warrior with ties to the San Jacinto Valley to lose his life. Born October 17, 1981 in Santa Ana, California, he and his family moved to San Jacinto in 1983 when Bryan was 2 years old. He graduated from San Jacinto High School in 2000. He entered the Army in April 2000 and arrived at Fort Campbell in November 2002. He had served three previous tours in Iraq, and his fourth tour in Iraq was coming to an end. He was due to arrive home on May 30th, in order to make his son's fifth birthday by May 31st, then he was to marry his fiancée Sandra on June 6th. He was assigned to the 1st Battalion, 502nd Infantry Regiment, 2nd Brigade Combat Team, 101st Airborne Division (Air Assault), United States Army, Fort Campbell, Kentucky. He was killed when an IED struck the vehicle he was riding in on April 29, 2008 in Baghdad, Iraq.

His mother Toni, said,

"The notification personnel came to my home when my oldest daughter (22 years old) was home with my grandkids and she called me and told me they were at the house for Bryan. My son was not married, so I was the primary person of notification. At the time, I was with my 16-year-old daughter at a truancy hearing. She had missed a couple days of school. In Tennessee, they take truancy very seriously, unlike California. We sold our house in California and moved to Tennessee. We were living in Clarksville at the time, and my son was stationed at Fort Campbell. My daughter's truancy got pushed way to the back when we told them about the phone call and we had to leave. The school took great pity on her for what had happened to her brother and nothing ever came of it, so my daughter likes to say that Bryan rescued her from any serious consequences for her truancies.

I didn't know what the outcome would be, so I called my husband on the way home from the truancy hearing. I didn't know what to expect. I remember telling my daughter while in the car that I never prayed so hard for one of my children to be hurt, because I didn't want him to be killed. I wanted him to just be hurt.

I came home and sent my daughter into the house to be with her sister and told her to shut the door. As I walked up to them, I knew immediately because one of them was a chaplain. The chaplain only comes for one reason, and all they said is that he had been killed. They didn't say much more. They have paperwork you have to fill out. The two of them just stayed at my house until my husband came home.

I was pretty numb when I heard about it, and I think I was in shock, because when I look back and think about the things I did at that time, I think, 'Why the hell did I do that?' I made a pot of coffee. I didn't have much to say. I hadn't really processed it, because I was in shock. I knew it to be true, but in my head, I don't think I had totally processed what actually happened. I remember my two daughters came to the table with me and the two military people just starred at each other. I don't really think I said much. I don't think I knew what to say. What I do remember is I did not fall apart, I did not break down, I did not lose it.

None of that happened, and I think that happened because my husband being a truck driver, I was always the one home taking care of things. He would be gone for as much as two weeks at a time. So, I knew I had to be strong for the kids, because I was all they had to keep things stable most of the time. I couldn't allow myself to fall apart. I was not going to give these guys any reason to call in any professional help, thinking I was crazy or losing it over this. I just knew I had to be strong for my kids.

My husband Bob was home within twenty minutes after telling him they were at the house. As soon as he got home they left. My husband raised Bryan. Bryan's stepdad was his dad.

This was Bryan's fourth deployment in Iraq, and living so close to his base, in a military town, his mother knew that it was not going to take long for word of his death to spread around town once the mandatory informational blackout was lifted after his next of kin were notified. Toni said:

"I didn't want his fiancée Sandra and her kids to find out about it from someone else in town. I wanted them to find out about it from my husband and me. So, I called her and told her she needed to come to my house and we told her.

Afterward we all just sat around in the living room and talked about him. Then, she left to go get her children to bring them back to the house.

My husband and I went to our bedroom to make some phone calls. I have an older son who, at the time, lived in Arkansas. He had to be called. My cousin was on the phone with him trying to keep him calm. I could hear him on the phone just losing it. He was hysterical.

All my family still lived in California and I had to let my mom know, so I called my brother at work to ask him to take care of all the notifications in California for me. As soon as I had to say the words to him that Bryan was killed in Iraq, I became very hysterical. I lost it. My brother said, 'I can't understand you. Let me talk to Bob.' So, I put Bob on the phone. My brother was very concerned for me. When I had to say that my son was killed in Iraq, that's when the reality set in that he was really gone.

I lost it for about five minutes then I pulled myself together and thought, 'No. You know what, I have to be strong. I have to do this for Bryan. I have to be strong for my daughters and grandkids.' I don't know why I felt that way.

They have paperwork you have to fill out immediately. It's difficult. One of the hardest parts about it for family members, whether you're the parents, or the wife, or whatever your circumstances are is the paperwork. It was weeks of paperwork. Even before he was flown out of Iraq it was three or four days, because everything was grounded due to paperwork."

Shortly before his death Bryan sent a picture home to his mother. It was him standing next to his Cougar safety vehicle that had substantial damage after triggering an IED. It was in for repairs. On the back of the photo, Bryan wrote: "Mama, they tried to blow me up, but I sure showed them." While the Cougar was being repaired, Bryan did his patrols in a regular flat bottom Humvee. His mother said:

"My son's vehicle was the last one and all the other vehicles were the safety type of vehicles. All the other vehicles drove over that IED and as soon as his Humvee went over it, it detonated. There were only two guys in the vehicle. He was the passenger in the front right seat. The driver was hurt, but he was okay. The IED was right outside the compound gates, and I believe his vehicle was targeted specifically, because they knew that it could be blown up. They blew him up. They blew my baby up."

Bryan's friend Joe was in the lead vehicle when the IED struck. After the blackout was lifted Bryan's mother was sitting at home on her computer when Joe popped up on instant messenger from Iraq. He said, "Momma, I ran back and tried to save him. I tried to save him. I tried so hard. I tried. I'm so sorry." Bryan and Joe were best friends.

Toni said:

"I was concerned about his best friend Joe's welfare who was out there. I knew it was going to devastate him. They had been roommates for most of their military careers. I remember thinking, 'Oh, poor Joey. I wished I could get to Joey, because he was just devastated.'"

"When they flew my son to Outlaw field near our home and his casket came off the plane. That was when it all became real to me that my son was gone. My husband and I were there, and I sheltered my children from all of that. I just felt they didn't need to experience all that.

My son is buried at Kentucky Veteran Cemetery in Oak Grove, Kentucky. He always told us he was going to be in the military until they kicked him out. He said when he retired from the military he was going to move back to Clarksville, Tennessee, buy a home, and that's where he was going to live, because he absolutely loved Clarksville, Tennessee. So, I buried him where he wanted to live.

He was buried on May 15th, and on May 17th my husband had a heart attack. And I remember being out in the hospital parking lot leaning on my car and I looked up at the sky and said, 'What did I ever do to you? I just buried my child. Why are you going to do this?' I think at that point I was just afraid that my husband was going to follow my son. I remember thinking that in less than a month I buried a child and I could be a widow. After that, I thought, 'Okay, you gotta pull yourself together, because you have kids at home and people that had to get to the airport who came out for the funeral who were going home the next day and I said I have to get it together now, because they really only have me.

My son's death certificate has the word 'Murdered' on it. They consider my son murdered.

When we got the autopsy report my husband and I went over it with our casualty assistance officer. The only thing I wanted to know is that he was killed instantly and did not suffer.

He was either killed when his neck was broken from the blast, or by all the shrapnel. I call it crap that was found in his heart — screws, bottle caps and other crap. He was also buried with no left arm. I don't know if they ever recovered his left arm, because I signed a piece of paper saying I did not want to be notified if, for some reason, they found his left arm. It was really unimportant to me. The only thing that made it difficult was because he did not have a left arm I could not have an open casket. According to military guidelines they have to be buried in their Class As and it has to fit as if they were alive wearing it and because he did not have a left arm they couldn't have an open casket. I wanted to see him. I wanted to see his face. So, that hurt me that I couldn't see him.

The two things that made me feel better is that he was killed instantly. He did not lay down and suffer and the person that set that IED was caught, sent to trial, and executed. If I could have gone to Iraq, I would have sat through the whole trial, but of course I couldn't. It took less than a month for them to find out who did it. His friend Joe told me on instant messenger that he and others were not allowed to be in on the investigation, because he never would have made it to trial. They would have killed him as soon as they found out who it was. They were not allowed to be involved in the investigation.

One of the most common questions I get asked is if I'm angry and I was never really angry. I was just the saddest I have ever been in my life, but it was never anger.

My husband and I believe that if you don't have people who are directly involved in the war then they're just forgotten. Unless you're out there among them or you're a part of them, they are forgotten. Nobody remembers these young men, like my son, who have been killed in Iraq and Afghanistan. The wars have been going on so long that the people are just numb to it. It's in the news all the time and that's just the way it is and unless you're a part of it you don't really think about it.

I try not to let it bother me and I also do believe that the Gold Star parents are far more forgotten than the widows and the children.

My son had one child and I don't ever want Tyler to ever be forgotten and I want people to know what his father sacrificed his life. As for us parents, people will say 'Oh, I'm sorry for your loss.' but sometimes I think the burden is far worse for the parents, because we're stuck. We have nowhere to move on to. You're not supposed to bury your children, and it's real hard as a parent to move on from that. I tell people somedays it's like it happened yesterday. I can tell you the conversation word for word that took place with my casualty assistant officer and my son will be gone nine years this year. It's tough and people don't realize that we sort of get stuck.

I have a daughter with Down Syndrome. Her and Bryan had a strong bond. He was going to be her caretaker when I could no longer care for her. She was eleven when he was killed, and they were best friends. They were very close. They had a bond ever since she was a baby. When they would see each other, their eyes would light up. They just loved each other so much. What kept me going after my husband had a heart attack was the thought of all these kids needing me."

Bryan had a park named after him on Lyon Street between Cottonwood and Esplanade in San Jacinto, California.

Bryan's military awards and decorations include:

The Army Commendation Medal with "V" Device
(2) Army Commendation Medals
The National Defense Service Medal
(2) Army Good Conduct Medals
The Iraqi Campaign Medal
The Global War on Terrorism Expeditionary Medal
The Global War on Terrorism Service Medal
The Kosovo Campaign Medal with Bronze Service Star
(2) Noncommissioned Officer Professional Development Ribbons
The Army Service Ribbon
(2) Overseas Service Ribbons
The NATO Medal
The Meritorious Unit Citation
The Ranger Tab
The Combat Infantry Badge
The Expert Infantry Badge
The Air Assault Badge
The Parachutist Badge
The Weapons Qualification, M4, expert

May 6, 2008

One week later, May 6, 2008, the eleventh loss would occur. It would be 19-year-old Army PFC Aaron Joseph Ward, of San Jacinto, California.

True Cost of Liberty - The Burden of Freedom

Staff Sgt. Bryan Eugene Bolander

Staff Sgt. Bolander with his son Tyler

Pfc. Aaron Joseph Ward

Chapter 11
Pfc. Aaron Joseph Ward

Joseph was born on April 28, 1989 in Portland, Oregon to Debbie and Paul Ward. The whole family moved to Sun City in Southern California in 1996, because the kids wanted to be closer to their grandparents. After renting a home in Sun City for a short while, Aaron's family bought a house twenty miles east in San Jacinto, California. While living in San Jacinto Aaron thoroughly enjoyed watching football, and his favorite team was the New England Patriots. He loved to skateboard. He liked to ride his BMX bicycle. He participated in wrestling for a short while. He played basketball through a community program. He did Cub Scouts, and he loved working on his car.

After graduating from Mountain View High School in San Jacinto, he was sent to boot camp in July 2007. Upon completing boot camp, he was assigned to the 170th Military Police Company, 504th Military Police Battalion, 42nd Military Police Brigade, Fort Lewis, Washington.

His uncle Gary said,

"After MP school, he came to visit us for two weeks and never once did I see him out of uniform. He was proud as a peacock to be walking around in that Army uniform. He loved his job. He went in a boy and they sent us home a man. He was a gung-ho kid. He was very patriotic. His uniform was always squared away. He was going to do whatever he had to do if it was going to help the mission. He was a hundred percent Army. He was a hundred percent MP. He loved being military police. He found his passion and it showed."

His mother Debbie said:

"When he was in Fort Lewis he called me and said, 'They are going to call you to talk to you and ask if you want me to go to Iraq', because he was my only son and the last one who could carry the Ward name. He said, 'Don't say anything that will keep me from going to Iraq. There are a lot of guys who need a break and I want to give them a break.' So, I said okay. It was what he really wanted to do more than anything else. Now, I wish I never said that."

Eager and confident, he arrived in Iraq in March 2008 and his mother said:

"When he was in Iraq, he called me every day and it was always the oddest times, and I was always sleeping. He would say, 'Good morning beautiful!' Of course, I would always talk to him. I would never say no."

Aaron was eighteen years old when he arrived in Iraq and all of his older comrades wanted to keep him safe. The older soldiers felt it was their duty to protect him from the enemy.

His uncle Gary said:

"They didn't just throw him into the fire. They felt it was their responsibility to watch over him. Some of the guys that were with him were from twenty-two years-old to twenty-six years old, and he was a baby to them. He had gone on other missions, but they made him stay in the vehicle. They watched over him for the first three months."

The MP's job was to post out and cordon off an area as a Marine unit would go into a building. They would watch for trouble outside of a building as the Marines went in to clear it. On Tuesday, May 6, 2008 Aaron's mother Debbie said:

"The whole day was off for me. I had just gone to the doctor and when I got home I was told by a neighbor that there was a guy in uniform looking for me at my house. I had a weird feeling something happened to Aaron. I called my sister and my dad and said something happened to Aaron, because I was told that there was a guy in uniform looking for me. My sister showed up and we had to wait a couple hours for them to come back. At about 5 p.m. I saw them walking up to my door. A soldier and a minister came to the front door and told me they regret to inform me Aaron was killed in Iraq. After hearing that I passed out. I actually fainted and fell right on the floor. My sister was there with me. She had called my dad and told him to come to the house. When he got to the house and found out Aaron was killed he had a heart attack on the spot. It was a mild one and he had to have stints put in. He doesn't remember the funeral at all. I think he blocked it out. It was the worst day of my life.

After I pulled myself together I called Aaron's dad and told him, but they had already called him on his cell phone and told him, which was horrible, because it was his birthday. Aaron was killed on his dad's birthday."

Being a close-knit family, word of Aaron's death spread quick among family members. Aaron's uncle Gary said:

"I was driving home from work and I got a phone call from my dad that told me there was an Army captain and a chaplain at my sister's house, and that Aaron was just killed. My heart just dropped. It made me sick to my stomach.

My sister was devastated. She was just devastated. She had a bad feeling after she spoke to her neighbor, because she was told there were two people in uniform looking for her. It was a rough couple of hours for her while she waited for them to come back."

After speaking extensively with members of Aaron's unit he was filled in on the details of Aaron's unit and the incident that took his life. His uncle Gary said:

"His unit was only going to be there another two and a half months, because they had already been there a while when he arrived. It was actually his first patrol where they let him get out of the vehicle. They just did a routine patrol and cleared a building. Everyone was loading back up when this guy came around the corner at the far end of the building with a full auto machine gun. He just held the trigger down. It's called a volley where they hold the trigger down and basically spray the area. They were loading back up, but they were still prepared. They fired back and it started a small arms battle right there. They didn't get him. He took off, and they went after him. Aaron and a sergeant happened to be over to the side. The sergeant got hit and Aaron took five shots to the body, but his Kevlar stopped the bullets from penetrating. A sixth shot got him just behind his left ear and that's what killed him. He was pretty much gone on impact. The corpsman assigned to him performed CPR and tried to revive him for thirty minutes, but he was gone on impact.

Aaron was killed on May 6th in Asad, Iraq one week after his nineteenth birthday. A lot of the guys that were with him when he was killed are feeling a lot of guilt, because he was so young.

They clearly saw the guy when he came around the corner and started shooting. Ironically, I got a report that three months later they got him. He was killed by the next group of guys that came in. They recognized him when they found him dead."

Aaron was flown home and landed at March Air Force Base on May 13, 2008. Aaron's mother Debbie said:

"Making the arrangements for him was horribly, horribly hard. When they brought him home it was so hard, a huge part of me was missing.

My whole family was there when they brought him home to the airport. His sister Samantha and I met the casket by the airplane and we laid across it and she looked at me and said, 'Mom, Aaron is afraid of the dark.' As a kid he always wanted the lights on at night. Even in high school he would keep the television on at night.

When we got him home, they drove him through Hemet, San Jacinto, and to his high school."

His funeral took place the next day on May 14, 2008. It began with a viewing service and Aaron's uncle Gary said:

"I regret seeing him in the casket. I wish I didn't. My wife refused to see him so she didn't. She wanted to keep the memory of him as the little kid that would come over and be the nonstop chatter box with fifty million questions."

His mother Debbie said:

"He had so many friends that came to his wake and funeral, and a lot of his favorite things were at the funeral. His sister sang 'Amazing Grace' and I don't know how she did it."

Aaron was finally laid to rest at Riverside National Cemetery in Riverside, California, and like all other Gold Star family members, Debbie's biggest fear was that her son would be forgotten. She said:

"My biggest fear was that Aaron would be forgotten. But he has a street named after him. He has a park named after him in San Jacinto. His high school band teacher bought a brick with his name on it and it's at the school. At Fort Lewis, Washington they have a beautiful memorial for all the MPs who have been killed in action and his name is on it."

His uncle Gary added:

"Up until 2012 to 2013 you would be amazed how many places no longer have the military discount. I can't help but think, 'Wow, how quickly you guys forget.' When it's politically correct, they do it, but after the fact it's too bad."

A week after Aaron was killed his sister, Samantha, found out she was pregnant. Debbie said:

"My daughter told me she was pregnant with my first granddaughter, Zoey, a week after Aaron's death. She has four girls now and she wanted a boy to name after her brother, so her fourth daughter she named Kimberlynn and gave her the middle name Aaron.

Aaron's recruiter Sgt. Lopez and his wife called me and asked if they could take me out to dinner, because they wanted to talk to me. They told me they were having a baby, and they found out it was a boy. They asked my permission to name their son's middle name Aaron. Of course, I said yes."

Like all Gold Star parents, the sudden loss of a child in war has a permanent and deep effect. Debbie's brother Gary said:

"My sister is different now. Part of her spirit is gone. She wanted to die when she found out. Her only son is gone and she wanted to die. If Debbie didn't have another child I believe my sister would not have survived. It was that bad. She's an inspiration to me, because if it were one of my kids I don't know that I would have survived. He was my nephew. I loved him to death. We were really tight.

I wear a dog tag around my neck that was around his boot when he was killed. I wear the Black Memorial bracelet in his memory and so does my son. I know how hard it hit me as an uncle, and I can't imagine or fathom how hard it would be if it was my own son. I talk to a lot of Gold Star parents, and I can't imagine how difficult it must be.

We're a long line of military. My uncle Wes and my uncle Billy were both Marines. Uncle Wes served in Vietnam. My dad served in both the Navy and the Army. My mom was in the Navy Reserves. I was in the Navy. My brother was in the Navy. My wife was in the Navy. My son is currently in the Navy. I have a nephew that's a chief in the Navy. Another nephew that is a sergeant in the Army. And Aaron. We firmly believe in this country. We all survived and we lost a 19-year-old. I'm a disabled vet myself, and I struggle with the fact that I survived, and he had to go.

Aaron was just a kid that was just happy to be here. He was an average kid. Never got into trouble. He was full of life and a happy kid. He was born with a natural smile, so he was always smiling. He and I talked a long time before he ever joined the military. He just felt it was his calling."

Aaron's mother said:

"I signed Aaron's papers that allowed him to go into the military and people ask me if I would sign them again and I would sign them again, because that's what he wanted.

They told me that Aaron volunteered for every mission he could get his hands on. They said he was a very good soldier. This is what he wanted to do more than anything."

One of Aaron's commanding officers called his mother from Iraq and asked her if she wanted anything. She said, "Yes, I want the American flag that was flying the day my son got killed." He said, "You got it." It came to her in the mail a few days later.

Debbie said:

"At first, I had so much hate in my heart for God and I wanted to kill the Iraqi people, and everything Iraqi so bad, but I don't feel that way anymore.

It took me a long time to move away from California, because I didn't want to leave my baby in that cemetery by himself."

On December 18, 2013, Aaron's sister Samantha posted this on the Facebook page:

In Loving Memory of PFC. Aaron J. Ward:

"Another Christmas without you here! This time of year is so hard to enjoy.

Thank God I have your three nieces to help me get through the holidays! I miss you more and more each day, I just wish I could hug you. You're my best friend baby brother, and my life will never be complete without my second half.

I love you so much, AJ! I just hope you know how proud I am of you, and how much I love you. God gave me my best friend when you were born, and made you my guardian Angel when he called you home. Merry Christmas my Angel, I miss your face!!"

On July 11, 2015 Aron's mother Debbie posted this on the same Facebook page.

"I miss my baby, I just want you back Aaron my heart is so broken, thank God for my Samantha she helps me more than she thinks."

June 18, 2008

Six weeks and one day later, on June 18, 2008, Hemet and San Jacinto would lose their twelfth warrior, 19-year-old Navy Hospitalman Marc Retmier.

Pfc. Aaron Joseph Ward

HN. Marc Allen Retmier

Chapter 12
HN. Marc Allen Retmier

"If I die, that's what happens. I can't stop fate and neither can you."
This was the answer Marc gave to his younger brother
Matthew after Matthew asked, "What if you die?"

Marc was born on September 28, 1988 in Fountain Valley, California. He was the firstborn child to Joy and Steve Retimier. Marc was named after his uncle Marc Robert Retmier, who passed away in 1976 at the age of nineteen while in the Navy on board the USS Enterprise. At the time of Marc's birth his parents were living with Joy's parents while they waited for their new home to be built in Menifee, California. Shortly after his birth the young family moved into their newly built home to start their new life.

Joy's father Dale Powers called Marc his retirement gift because Marc was born around the time Dale retired. This allowed Dale and Joy's mother Lois to spend quality time with Marc. Marc was colicky after his birth so Dale would take mark to his home lay him on his chest while seated in his recliner and rub Marc's back to help him get to sleep. He also did this to allow Joy and Steve to get some rest.

At the age of two Marc's brother Matthew was born, and he also had colic. When Joy came home from the hospital Dale and Lois picked Matthew up so Joy could get some much-needed rest. Once they left, two-year-old Marc dialed 911 and said to the operator, "Bubby and Papa took my baby brother." The police came to the house to check on the situation, and Joy had to explain what happened. They all had a chuckle.

Marc called Dale "Papa" and would always help him do work around their property. Dale always made sure to pay Marc. When Marc was two and a half, Dale, while doing some work on the property, would take a piece of two-by-four wood and drill undersized holes in it then place larger nails in the holes and let Marc hammer the nails into the wood. Dale always made sure that Marc felt like he was doing something useful and meaningful.

Lois made sure to have Marc help her when she was in the kitchen. On numerous occasions, she would have Marc help her bake chocolate chip cookies.

This was something Marc would come to love doing himself, and he always remembered the love he felt from Lois while she taught him how to bake cookies. When he was in Afghanistan, he sent Lois an email reminiscing and thanking her for making all those chocolate chip cookies with him. It was a happy memory he hung onto.

Dale and Lois would take Marc camping for a month-long trip near Parker, California along the Colorado River. When three-year-old Marc was informed that they were going to have to head back home to Hemet, he said, "No, never, ever, ever."

When Dale and Lois would drive places, Marc would sit in the back seat of their car. This is where Lois taught him how to sing the songs "Achy Breaky Heart" and "Money, Money, Money, Money."

Dale would take Marc to the Perris Airport and the owner of the airport would allow Marc to sit in the seat of an ultralight parked on the property. Four-year-old Marc began to say, "This is my ultralight."

At about the age of five Marc began to show an interest in playing "Army." He would play Army with his neighbors on a regular basis. His grandfather Dale took him to the store and bought him military clothing, play guns and other supplies to help Marc's play time be more fun.

When Marc was eight the Retmiers' third and final child, Mason, was born. Two years later the family moved the fifteen miles to Hemet, California in order to be closer to Dale and Lois who also moved to Hemet. Marc began fifth grade at Fruitvale Elementary School then went on to Acacia Middle school for sixth, seventh, and eighth grades. It was around middle school that Marc began to show an interest in riding bicycles and skateboards.

Once he finished middle school, he went on to West Valley High School for his freshman and sophomore year. He lettered in varsity swimming his freshman year and played football for the West Valley Mustangs. He was a successful safety on defense. His father Steve said:

> "I remember when he made his first interception as a free safety with West Valley High School Mustangs. He was tackled pretty hard afterwards, but when he got up I could see a huge smile through his face mask."

For his junior year, he transferred to Hemet High School. After part of the way through his senior year at Hemet High an insatiable desire to get on with his future motivated him to transfer from Hemet High to Alessandro Adult School in order to graduate early. That way he was able to fulfill his goal of finishing school and joining the Navy sooner rather than later.

While growing up Marc was an active skateboarder, snowboarder, surfer, and free style motocross dirt jumper. There were many pictures taken of Marc doing tricks on his motorcycle while he was flying through the air. According to his grandfather, 'He was a thrill seeker who enjoyed the adrenaline rush.' "

Marc was sent to North Chicago, Illinois to the Recruit Training Command (RTC) Bootcamp for all naval personnel. After his basic training, he went on to train at Fort Bragg, North Carolina, then Camp Lejeune, North Carolina. After completing this training, he was given orders to serve at the National Naval Medical Center in Bethesda, Maryland. This was exactly what Marc wanted for his choice of location. In the beginning, Marc was caught between wanting to be a pilot and a doctor. Being an adrenaline junky he loved the thought at the thrill of flying. A compassionate human being, he loved the thought of helping people in need. In the end, his compassionate side won out and Marc set his sights on becoming a medical doctor.

He strongly felt that his experience as a Navy Corpsman would provide for an excellent transition into medical school when his time in the Navy was completed. At this point, Marc's life goal was to become a doctor.

Wanting to experience the adrenaline of war, Marc volunteered for a mission in Iraq. When that Marine Corps deployment mission was canceled he then volunteered for a mission in Afghanistan. As a result, Marc was sent to Afghanistan in December of 2007. His father and grandfather drove him to the airport that morning. His father Steve said:

> "We had breakfast at McDonalds that morning, and just before he boarded the plane, I gave him a bigger hug than usual. Something just didn't feel right to me this time. I told Dale that something didn't feel right as we watched him board the plane. Dale said, 'Nothing can happen to him.' We followed the plane down as it taxied for takeoff then we watched it disappear into the clouds. I just didn't have a good feeling about it this time."

Marc was assigned to the Army's Provincial Reconstruction Team Sharana, stationed in the northern Paktika province of Afghanistan. The Provincial Reconstruction Team (PRT) consisted of eighty personnel, forty of which were military whose main purpose was to provide security and the other forty were a mixture of civil engineers, naval personnel, civil affairs personnel, and U.S. and agriculture personnel. The Provincial Reconstruction Team's main mission was to go through local Afghanistan governments and gain their permission and support in order to help the Afghans through governance, security, construction, agriculture, and medicine. Marc's position was to help provide medicine to any locals, villagers or military personnel who needed it.

On June 18, 2008, the Provincial Reconstruction Team was in Zerok, a small village in the northern Paktika province of Afghanistan. About twenty members of the team were about two kilometers from a small temporary compound that the 1st of the

503rd, 101st Airborne Division were occupying. They were conducting a Key Leader Engagement (KLE). A Key Leader Engagement is when leaders from Afghan villages and towns meet with the commanders of the Provincial Reconstruction Team. The Commanding Officer of the security force of the Provincial Reconstruction Team, 1st Lt. Brian Kinkade, said:

> "We were conducting a KLE about two kilometers from the 101st Airborne Division's compound. A KLE can last anywhere from one to three hours. However, this particular one was cut short after about an hour due to continuous indirect fire the 101st Division's compound was receiving. We drove back to the compound. When we arrived, I instructed the men to go ahead and eat lunch. They went into a small Afghan government building the 101st let us use. This building was about twelve feet by twenty feet on the inside and there were about fifteen personnel that went inside to have lunch. I was sitting in my truck about twenty feet in front of the building using my blue force tracker computer system to send reports to headquarters about the KLE and the indirect fire that had been coming in periodically throughout the morning. About fifteen or twenty minutes into the men's lunch break we heard an explosion strike the ground a few hundred feet beyond the small structure the men were in. Then we heard a second explosion land short of the building. At this point, Platoon Master Sergeant Holmes, who was in the truck with me, said, 'I should tell the men to put flak jackets on and get into the armored vehicles.' I said, 'Yes, go do that.' Master Sergeant Holmes went into the building. He wasn't in there for more than a few seconds when I heard a third explosion as I was looking down at my computer. When I looked up I could see that the building the men were in took a direct hit. I jumped out of my truck and made it to the building in about three seconds. When I got to the door Staff Sergeant Mike Kacer was walking out. His left arm was basically severed from his body, and from his nose down it looked like his face had been through a meat grinder. His jaw was basically lying on his chest.

I sat him down and told him he looked okay and he was going to be fine. I began to put a tourniquet on his left arm when Spc. Evan Debiassa came out of the building dazed and concussed, but with no serious visual wounds. I instructed Spc. Debiassa to finish with SSG Kacer's tourniquet. As I entered the building I could hear screaming and moaning. The next person I encountered was a soldier who was assigned to us just for that mission. He was walking around under his own power, but he had a hole in his cheek and I could see his teeth. As I continued in, the next one I saw was Petty Officer First Class Ross Toles. He was sitting on his cot on the right side of the room with his feet toward the center and his back against the wall as if he was reading a book, but I could immediately tell by the nature of his wounds he was deceased. There was nothing I could do, so I continued on with my assessment. Hospitalman Marc Retmier was the next one I came to. From the time of the blast to the time I made it to Marc was about sixty seconds. He also was on the right side of the room laying down on his cot with his head toward the wall and his feet toward the center. I put my ear to his nose and mouth listening for breathing as I looked down the length of his body to see if I could see any rising and falling of his chest. As I was doing this I was also searching for a pulse on his neck, but there was nothing. No pulse and no breathing. He also was deceased. There was nothing I could do at this point. He had lost a large amount of blood.

It was obvious to me that the enemy was ranging in on our position and the way it usually works is once they find the range to the target they release a barrage of artillery or rockets. While in the building I have never been so scared in all my life, because I was completely expecting that barrage to hit us at any second, but it never came."

Upon further investigation, it was determined that a piece of shrapnel severed the artery that ran down the inside of Marc's right leg. Marc died from massive bleeding through his right femoral artery. Marc would be the 500th Californian killed from the wars in Iraq and Afghanistan.

In their "Immediate Release," the Department of Defense wrote:

The Department of Defense announced today the death of two sailors who were supporting Operation Enduring Freedom.

Hospitalman Marc A. Retmier, 19, of Hemet, Calif., and Petty Officer First Class Ross L. Toles III, 37, of Davison, Mich.

Died June 18 as a result of wounds suffered from an enemy rocket attack in northern Paktika province, Afghanistan.

They were assigned to Provincial Reconstruction Team Sharana in Afghanistan.

On June 18, 2008, Marc's mother, Joy, arrived home from work and went into her room to put her pajamas on. As she was finishing up, her 11-year-old son, Mason, answered a knock at the door. Standing outside were three sailors in uniform. Mason went to his mom and said, "Mom, there are three men wearing uniforms at the door." Joy said:

"At that moment, I knew. I hurried to the door and when I saw them they didn't have to say a word. I began to cry hysterically. They never send men in uniform to your home to tell you your son is wounded."

The men came into the house with a hysterical Joy. After a brief moment, Joy called her father Dale first. Dale said:

"When I answered the phone, Joy was hysterical and I could not make out what she was saying.

I knew it had something to do with Marc, because the only time she had ever been that upset is when Marc wrecked his vehicle at the age of sixteen from reckless driving. He didn't hurt himself, or anybody else, but the police took him to jail anyway. Then through all her blubbering and screaming I heard her say, 'Daddy, daddy, daddy, Marky is dead.' When I heard those words, it was like the end of my life. Lois and I immediately jumped in our vehicle and high tailed it to their house."

About this same time 11-year-old Mason called his father, Steve, at work in Laguna Hills and said, "Daddy, daddy, Marky is dead." Steve said:

"I said to Mason, 'That is not even funny Mason. Put your mother on the phone.' But I could hear her screaming hysterically in the background. My heart just dropped to the floor. I knew it was real. I said to Mason that I was on my way home. I stepped out of the office and went about ten feet into the warehouse where I worked and my knees gave out, and I collapsed to the floor and began crying. I called my coworkers to come over and help me. They thought I was having a heart attack. When they got to me, they helped me sit in a chair, and I told them what happened, and they started to cry and hug me. After a while they helped me back to my feet. I said to them I had to drive home and they said that I was not driving myself anywhere. I carpooled with my former brother-in-law. He drove me home. It was the longest hour and a half drive I have ever had in my whole life. The anticipation of what I was going to find at home was killing me. It was pretty much what I expected at home."

Joy called her son Matthew. Matthew said:

"I was at a friend's house playing pool when my phone rang. I wasn't going to answer it because I was in a pretty heated pool game that I wanted to win, but something inside me told me I should answer this call. When I picked it up, my mom was hysterical and crying into the phone and I couldn't understand her at first. Then I heard her say Marc is dead. I dropped the phone and my whole body went numb, then my knees gave out and I collapsed to the floor and began to cry hysterically. I told my friends what happened, and then I drove home as quickly as I could."

Marc's body was flown home from Bethesda Hospital in Maryland and he was laid to rest on June 25, 2008 in Corona del Mar, California at the Pacific View Cemetery. His plot overlooks the ocean and he was placed near his uncle whom he was named after. His parents made the choice to put the majority of the life insurance money they received toward his funeral. They felt it was his money and they wanted him to have the best funeral they could possibly give him.

Like all families who have lost a loved one the Retmiers' burden is a day-by-day struggle. Marc's grandfather Dale says, "It's out of order. We should never have to bury our children, or our grandchildren."

Marc's mother Joy says:

"The pain never goes away. I have good days then I will see a picture of Marc and I will start to cry, or I will go smell his clothes and I will start to cry. I will ask, 'Why, why, why? What did I do to deserve this? It has really made me lose faith in God. Where was God at the moment that rocket killed my son?"

Marc's father, Steve, said:

"Why our son? What happened here? He was a good boy, and there was no reason for it to happen. He was giving help to those people.

I'm very bitter about it. Those bastards took my son away. It has affected my family something fierce. It's hard for me to see people in uniform. It takes my breath away. It makes me short of breath every day when there is something that reminds me of him. I'm very proud of my son. He put his all into it. I said, 'Put your all into it.' He said, 'I will dad, I will.'

I'm just an average guy, and an average worker. Now my son's dog tag hangs from my rearview mirror. I touch it every morning I go to work and tell him I love him and I tell him I love him every day I leave work. A lot of hopes and dreams were ripped out of my head. He was going to be a pilot and a doctor.

I feel alone now. Nobody asks about him anymore. It's a very lonely feeling— out of sight, out of mind. Nobody asks me about Marky anymore. I feel very alone, my family does.

The pain doesn't end. It's not as intense as it used to be, but it hurts every day. It doesn't end. He's not on this earth anymore, but supposedly he's in heaven. It makes me really question heaven and God. I don't disbelieve, but it makes me really question. It's a horrible thing. It really is."

Both of Marc's parents feel upset for signing the papers allowing him to join at the age of seventeen. They wish they would have waited for him to do it himself when he was eighteen. They both believe that might have made a difference.

Approximately one month after Marc's death, Evan Debiassa, who was in the building with Marc at the time the rocket hit, told Lt. Brain Kinkade about a conversation he and Marc had a few days before Marc's death. Marc told Evan he would rather die in place of Evan since Evan had a newborn son back home. Marc said since he didn't have a wife or children back home, he would rather die for Evan, because Evan's son would need his father. The day of the incident Marc went into the building and sat on Evan's cot to eat lunch. Normally, being somewhat territorial, Evan would have told Marc to get off of his cot, but this time Evan said he let it be because he just didn't feel like saying anything.

Instead, Evan sat on the floor next to Marc. When the blast occurred, Marc was between Evan and the blast, shielding Evan from any deadly shrapnel. When Evan approached Lt. Kinkade with this story, Evan said:

> "I now know why Marc sat in my cot instead of me. He was giving me the opportunity to be the best father I could possibly be to my son and that's exactly what I am going to do."

The ramifications from that single attack are a perfect testament to the Burden of Freedom's lasting effects. The collateral damage caused by this incident was physically injurious to survivors and psychologically traumatic to comrades. This single rocket attack, that took the lives of Marc Retmier and Ross Toles, has had a lifelong effect on survivors. Michael Kacer survived the attack, but his life would never be the same, and the burden he carries will be with him for the rest of his life.

HN. Marc Allen Retmier

Marc Retmier administering first aid to an Afghan child.

Chapter 13
Staff Sgt. Michael Kacer

Unlike Gold Star families, relatives of wounded warriors do not have to face the death of their loved one. However, they do have to face a physically altered loved one. Michael Kacer survived the rocket attack that took the lives of Hospitalman Marc Retmier and Officer First Class Ross Toles, but the scars he does bare are a true testament to the high cost of freedom.

Mike was born on January 3, 1982 at St. Joseph's Hospital in Carbondale, Pennsylvania. He was the son to Betsy Barrera and Michael Kacer Sr. Michael Sr. served two tours of duty in Vietnam as a medic with the Green Beret Special Forces and when Mike Jr. was eleven years old, he watched his father in action.

"I saw my dad save somebody's life from heat stroke, and I wanted to do something like that. It wasn't a big deal to him, but it was a big deal to me. I wanted to live a life with a positive impact."

Michael Sr. was instrumental in getting Mike Jr. on the right path after Jr. began hanging out with a partying crowd his sophomore year in high school.

"My dad kept telling me that I had to find myself, and that he did not want to see me go down the wrong path. I asked him what a good route would be and he said the military is always an option."

On his father's advice, Mike decided to join the National Guard during his junior year in high school. On June 12, 1999, the summer between his junior and senior years, he went to basic training in the Split-Option Enlistment Program. Half the training was completed the first summer and the second half was completed the summer after graduation. He signed up for six years.

Mike's first deployment was to Bosnia for fourteen months from January 3, 2002 to March 3, 2003 as part of a peacekeeping mission.

> "We were there to make sure nothing spurred up between the three countries. The peace keeping troops we replaced were sent to Iraq."

After returning home in March 2003, it would not be until December 2003 that Mike was told his second deployment would be to Iraq, and on February 22, 2004, he was sent off to the hostile nation. He was assigned to the 1st Marine Expeditionary Division at camp Falluja, which was less than five minutes south of the infamous city of Falluja. He was part of the infantry unit whose job was to provide security for the Explosive Ordinance Detail missions inside Falluja. Mike never experienced any serious threats while serving his time in Iraq, but fourteen months in Iraq had an impact.

Upon returning home from Iraq in April 2005, he spent the next month in Combat Debriefing. It was to help him readjust back to civilian life. Mike said:

> "It did help me. I knew two guys who got out and could not adjust. Alcoholism and divorce came into their lives. I had a good support network from my family. When I would get angry they would bring it to my attention, and I used it to get me through some tough times with my PTSD."

In April of 2007, a notification came in that said his unit would be going to Afghanistan. Mike's wife did not want him to go.

"My wife said she did not want me to volunteer, but if they took me she would stay by my side. So, I lied and said they took me. I didn't want the new guys to go without my experience. I would have felt terrible if something happened to them."

As the plans unfolded, all of his guys were split up anyway, and Mike left the United States on February 27, 2008, and arrived in Baghran, Afghanistan the first week of March. He would become part of the Provincial Reconstruction Team's security unit.

On June 18, 2008, Mike, Marc Retmier and about thirteen others were taking their lunch break in the small building where Marc and Ross were killed. They all removed their body armor. The two-feet thick walls provided enough protection for them while they ate their MREs (Meals Ready to Eat). According to one naval investigator, Robert Rockwell, "It was a one in a million shot" from a Chinese-made 107mm rocket that hit the windowsill then fell through the window and landed on the floor. Staff Sergeant Mike Kacer said:

"I was seated in the right rear corner of the room. I heard the whistle of a rocket, and I could tell by the sound of it that it was going to be close. It hit the ground just beyond the wall that was right up to the back side of our building. I said out loud to the rest of the guys, 'That one was close!' Then I remember hearing the whistle of the next rocket and I knew I just needed to get out of the building. I got up and started running for the door. The next thing I remember was seeing a flash of light then I thought I was dead, because I couldn't feel anything, or hear anything. I was the only one standing in the room. Everybody else was laying down. I looked around the room trying to find my own body then I realized I wasn't dead. I went back to the cot I was sitting on and sat down. I thought I was okay until I saw a quarter size hole in my abdominal area and thought it was right where my stomach was, then I saw my jaw swing out in front of my face. I realized I was seriously wounded. The shock started to set in almost immediately. I thought to myself, 'I'm seriously wounded, I'm bleeding out, I'm going into shock and the medevac is about an hour away. I don't think I'm going to make it.' I remember walking out of the building and interacting with Lt. Kinkade. Lt. Kinkade was telling me that I looked good, and I was going to be okay. I knew I didn't look good with my jaw swinging out in front of me, and I did not think I was going to be okay, so with the best sense of humor I had left I said through what was left of my mouth, 'With all due respect sir, fuck you'. After that I think I was going in and out of consciousness, because I only remembered some things like them sending the men who could walk to the vehicles then I remember being put on the helicopter."

His left arm had mostly been severed except for some pieces of tissue still connected to his body, and according to Lt. Brian Kinkade:

"From his nose down, it looked like his face had been through a meat grinder. His jaw was basically lying on his chest."

Michael's next memory occurred four days later, on June 22, when they pulled him out of his drug induced coma at Walter Reed Army Medical Center in Washington D.C.

"The first thing I noticed was severe cotton mouth. There was a cup of water next to my bed. I kept reaching for it with both hands and it kept spilling. I didn't know my left arm was missing. I also could not get any water in my mouth because my jaw was wired shut and I didn't know that. It wasn't until the nurse told me that I knew, then my family got upset, because they wanted to be the ones to tell me about my arm."

Surgeons amputated his arm in Germany before he was flown to Walter Reed. They also had to redo his emergency colostomy that was done prior to sending him to Germany. The colostomy was the result of a piece of shrapnel striking him in the abdomen and severing his intestine. The doctors completely opened his abdomen in order to repair him and he had to carry a colostomy bag for the next seven months.

With his jaw wired shut from being broken in three places, a severely swollen tongue, and two collapsed lungs, Mike had to breathe through a trachea tube. For the first three days after coming out of his coma, communication was difficult. He said:

"Since I couldn't talk I tried writing, but everything came out jumbled. I couldn't coordinate what I was writing and what I was thinking. It just came out making no sense so I started using hand signals to communicate, like pointing at my mouth when I was thirsty."

When his mind eventually cleared, he was able to communicate through writing, but due to his wired jaw and trachea, verbal communication was not possible. It took him two weeks to learn how to control his vocal chords while plugging the hole on the end of the trachea tube in order for him to be able to speak again. He would have to do this for the next five months. This was to ensure that his recovered collapsed lungs would not cause any serious problems for him.

With plenty of time to think, Mike was wondering how much his life was going to change. Losing his limb was beginning to weigh on him. He wasn't sure how he was going to manage or even deal with such a loss. That is until he was moved from ICU to his regular room. While his sister Ariane was rolling him down the hallway in a wheelchair his friend from high school, Earl Granville, was a few doors down in his own room with his own injuries. They both joined the same National Guard unit at the same time and they were both deployed to Afghanistan. Earl was a gunner on a Humvee that drove over a double-stacked anti-tank mine fifteen days before Mike's incident. On June 3, 2008, Earl lost his left leg a few inches above the knee. When Earl saw Mike in the hallway, he said:

"Hey Mike! Come here! I want you to meet Steve the stump." as he held his left leg up.

Mike said, "That was probably one of the biggest and best things that ever happened to me. I couldn't do anything but laugh at that point."

That single incident shifted Mike's perception to a positive mindset and he said:

"It really came down to what I made of it. When I asked him how he could say that about his leg, he said, 'Hey, at least I have my life.' He was completely right."

This encounter seemed to give Mike a way to handle nearly anything, even when his wife informed him in the hospital that his injuries would be too much for her to handle, and she did not wish to be married to him any longer. The two had been together a total of five years and when Mike was well enough to leave the hospital, he and his wife filed for divorce just three days short of their one-year wedding anniversary.

Earl's comment really helped give Mike have the attitude necessary to carry him through his rehab. For ten months Mike had his jaw wired shut, and he had to eat a liquid diet through a straw. When the wires were removed, it took him another seven months before he could fully open his mouth. Over half of his teeth had been knocked out by the shrapnel that struck the left side of his face and nearly ripped his jaw off. They could not make a mold until he could open his mouth entirely. From the time of the injury to the time Mike had all of his teeth back in his mouth was two years. In the meantime, Mike made the most of it. He became a member of the Achilles Wounded Warrior Freedom Team, which is part of Achilles International, whose mission is to successfully guide disabled individuals towards the completion of extreme physical events such as marathons and triathlons. Since becoming a member in September 2008, Mike has completed three five-mile runs called "Hopes and Possibilities," one Disney half marathon, which was his first event in January of 2009, one Detroit half marathon, and eight full marathons. He also has plans to continue with these types of events with no end in sight.

For being a member of Achilles International, Mike and his nephew Isaiah were invited to a Yankee's baseball game at Yankee Stadium. On Friday, June 24, 2011, in the first inning Yankee's outfielder, Curtis Granderson, hit a pop-up foul ball just to the right of the Colorado Rockies dugout. The ball took a bounce back toward the stands. When Mike saw the ball heading in his direction he leaned over the glass railing and caught the ball in his hat then handed it to his nephew. The crowd let out a loud and long cheer for the one-armed vet. His catch made it into ESPN's top five plays and Fox News gave him an interview with his nephew at his side. The catch and the interview can be seen on YouTube under "Wounded Vet Catches Foul Ball With Hat at Yankee Game." Mike retired from the National Guard and has dedicated a large portion of his time to Achilles Wounded Warrior Freedom Team.

Chapter 14
CM2. Tyler Flower

Petty Officer First Class Ross Toles, who was killed along with Marc Retmier, gave up his trip home so fellow sailor Tyler Flower could go home for a two-week break.

"He (Ross Toles) took me off the mission without even asking me. Not only did he give me his flight home, but he took my mission."

Born June 2, 1984 in Napa, Idaho, Tyler joined the Navy in hopes of avoiding war in Iraq or Afghanistan, but fate would have him sent to Afghanistan as a mechanic in a Construction Battalion. He was a CB.

"It was the day I flew out of our main base for my two-week break that they were both killed, the day I was leaving. The others knew about it, but they said not to let me know so it would not ruin my trip home.

I found out about it on the return trip to Afghanistan. I met up with two of the Army guys from my unit in Kuwait before we headed back to Afghanistan. It was a dark night. We were sitting in a little hut, smoking cigarettes when they said something about it, and I said, 'What are you talking about?' The two of them looked at each other and said, 'You didn't hear?' They told me what happened. They were up in Zerok and had rockets walked in on them. One of them clipped the windowsill and sprayed the room with shrapnel and the concussion.

Of course, I went through all the grief steps, first shock, then denial, then anger. I had a grudge about Marc and Toles. That grudge, that hurt and that pain led me to that next deployment."

That next deployment would be a year and a half after the deaths of his friends. He spent a significant amount of time with U.S. Navy Seals at the end of 2009 as a mechanic. He would remain with the Seals until July 2013.

"In March 2011, I had my first engagement with the Seals. One of the things Naval Special Warfare does is instantly dominate the target with extreme violence. I turned to extreme violence as my medication. I wanted to do bad things to bad men. It kind of became my outlet for the rage I felt over the loss of Marc and Ross. I enjoyed the adrenaline, it felt good, and when the bullets were flying I smiled. I thrived on the violence of my actions, and that changes a man over time. Eleven months of running and gunning in fields and villages and things happen that you question when you get back to a real civilization. It's tricky trying to adjust.

When you prep your mind and body for combat it changes you, and you might not even notice it until you come back home. Combat experience is not the single problem. It is the way you are changed through the years of training, extended combat exposure, and unknown amounts of time away from your loved ones all while seeing very traumatic events which leads to the problems. Normal is no more for those men and women who go through all this.

Guys like me who had to get stuck in some shitty situations in villages, you're fine until you come home and then you try to mitigate risk in the civilian world and it takes a long time to adjust. The world becomes a scary place to traverse. My perception of the world has changed. My reactions to sights, sounds and my way of thinking, adapting, and handling issues have changed.

The skills I learned through all my training and experience don't go away. These skills helped keep me alive over there, so they don't just go away. The skills I'm talking about that I can't get rid of now is if I see a fighting age male I first look at his eyes to see where they are looking. I see his hands second, and if they are clean I'm looking at the waistline, looking for a bulge.

I want to see where his eyes are looking, because then I know what his intent is, or where he's going next and that's why I don't do good in crowds. It's exhausting, and there's a lot of anxiety, because I need to track what's going on around my family, so I'm tracking target A, B, C, D and I have six more behind me. I don't like anybody behind me, especially a fighting age male, because I need my family to be secure.

It's almost like you're constantly on guard. You're waiting for something to pop off, because that's how it was over there. We do a lot of things to mitigate risk and that stays with you especially if it helped save your life over there."

Every war creates carnage that imprints on the memory. These imprints may fade over time, but they never completely vanish. The distress from the experience can sear into the mind of the witness, and resurface when they are asleep, or any other time. Tyler said:

"Bodies after someone dies— the eyes are very cold, and the body can be contorted. Killing, seeing death, and many other cold aspects of war never leave the witness's mind. Ready to pop up and haunt the person at any time, or in any place. For me it has been in my sleep many times. In one of my reoccurring dreams I see my family's mangled bodies lying awkwardly on the battlefield, looking so much like the men who suffered from the barrel of our weapons. Their red and white insides displayed out as if they needed a breath of fresh air in that summer sun; cold dilated eyes still open like they are watching their own death throes in terror.

In another dream, I don't see the faces of men or Americans running around in their body armor. Instead, it's my baby girl bleeding out in a little uniform with little body armor, and I wake up sweating and crying. My biggest thing is the dreams and the night. Nights get lonely and dark pretty quick. That's the burden for men like me.

The dream I would have about Marc and Ross was one of me watching them training is the best way I can describe it, almost peaceful, very quiet.

It was like watching them on a movie or a video, watching them walk up a mountain or down a trail, but then I would wake up with bad feelings. The PTSD would not let me shake those bad feelings. They wouldn't go away. I just couldn't shake that cold mortal feeling.

When someone dies or when you watch their life end, it's a cold mortal feeling, especially if it's someone on your side or an innocent. I wish I could articulate exactly how it is but how do you describe the color orange to someone who has never seen orange? A good way to try and describe it is when you're trained and ready to go to war and you have your first shots fired at you, or something goes boom real close for the first time. You realize how mortal you really are. You're snapped back to reality. You feel very mortal really quick.

My nightmares are more random now, but the first couple years they were often, almost nightly. I had a recurring one where I was in Afghanistan where at first, I would just get shot and die. I would feel it and then I would feel myself twitching out, or dying. Then it would come back another night and go further to where I would get shot, and before I died I would have enough time to ask for forgiveness. Not for what I did in Afghanistan, but for life in general. I couldn't shake the feeling of that one when I would wake up. It would hit me hard.

The one with Marc, or Toles, going through some of the training we went through in Fort Bragg was more of a melancholy dream that would leave me with a feeling that I couldn't shake, and it would stay with me all day. The one of me dying was a real deep, dark, ice cold anxiety feeling in the pit of my stomach.

The conversion from war to civilian life can be a difficult transition for the combat veteran. The hypervigilance necessary to stay alive in a war zone does not simply turn off when a veteran returns home. As a result, normal living can be perceived as an overwhelming emotional maze.

"It's everything that gets me. Marc, Ross, being over there, anxiety, the stress from the PTSD.

I worry about my own kids, and that's what seems to get me now because I don't trust this world. My family is beautiful, and I don't care what happens to me, but I love my family so much that I just want them to be safe in this world that I don't trust.

When my wife does her 12-hour night shifts as an RN I don't have a second set of eyes or ears to know what something might be, or what a certain sound is, so I have the door locked. I have a shotgun posted by the bed stand. I've got a gun in the front closet by the door, and one on the fridge so that no matter what happens I have layers of defense. My wife knows where each one is and how to use them, and where to use them, because when I'm not there those defenses will be layered, and my family will be protected. All that training you go into to be victorious in battle is not something you just turn off. I understand that there are not just bad people that are just going to come and hurt me for no reason. The chances are slim, but still, I can't just turn that off. I can't have that security lacking, because my life depended on it for so long.

I can still hear his (Marc) songs, or see something that reminds me of him. Luckily it happens when I'm alone. I'll cry maybe six times a week still.

One of the things that messes with me the most is the memory of when kids got hurt. When I was with the Seals there was an IED meant for us, but a station wagon hit it, and a six-year-old girl's head went rolling, and the Taliban didn't clean that up, we did. Or, I remember the 4-year-old boy with burned up legs that looked like two little logs that had been in the fire overnight. He was screaming, and the medics were helping him in a cement building, a bombed-out school house, in the second village we hit and we were being shot at. We had an 18- hour fire fight with the Taliban. They didn't appreciate us being at one of their most remote safe havens in Northern Afghanistan, so when the bullets were flying they couldn't take the child outside. That kid screamed for many hours and now when my daughter is teething or crying for some other reason it takes me right back to that screaming kid, and I have to snap myself out of it."

War has always been brutal. When humans face off in battle their lives are at stake. As a result, human compassion takes a back seat and a primitive instinct to survive takes over. This instinct makes the warrior do whatever he has to do to stay alive regardless of compassion. Warriors fighting for their lives can have no compassion. But once the battle is over and the veteran returns home, this primitive instinct gradually fades to the background, and human compassion resurfaces, which can cause the veteran to feel some remorse from their war experiences.

> "I don't know how I'll be judged in the next life. Some things happened to some bad men. I had to do a few things that I struggle with now, and who's to say that they were bad men and I wasn't. I was in another person's home land. How many times has history judged people to be barbarians, or to be animals when I'm sure those men were doing what they needed to do and felt patriotic about it? They thought they were doing what is right."

Since September 11, 2001, America has mainly been fighting to keep Americans safe from our enemies, both foreign and domestic. President Bush decided to go into Afghanistan and Iraq to take the fight to the enemy and stop them at their point of origin, instead of waiting for them to breach our shores again. However, over the years, it appears the toughest obstacle American forces need to overcome is the enemies' deeply embedded cultural conditioning that has controlled their way of thinking for many centuries now.

> "Americans don't understand how different the cultures are. In Afghanistan, if you have something that the next guy doesn't, or your neighbor doesn't, then you're a better man than him. If he has something that you don't have, and you take it from him then you're a better man, because you have it now. One time they wanted me to give them some barriers to block off this little river.

When I asked them why, they said they wanted to redirect the water to their village, and when we asked them about the other village that would lose their flow of water as a result, they said if they want water for their crops, or for themselves to live off they would have to pay us. And we said, 'If someone came and took your village's Wi-Fi what would you do?' And they said, 'Oh, we would go kill them.' So we said, 'If we do this for you what do you think that village is going to do?' Well they will come and fight us, but we'll kill them, and that means we can have what they have, and we're better.

There was also an incident where I saw a woman whose husband didn't want her anymore, because he had a couple other women. He said that she was an adulteress , so they took her out into the middle of nowhere, cut her ears and nose off, and left her. It's a different culture out there."

Advanced societies would never allow this type of treatment to be imposed on its people. However, people in advanced societies may not fully comprehend the harsh realities that citizens of third world nations endure daily. They can never truly grasp it like those who are living it. They also do not entirely comprehend the experiences our military personnel have encountered, and it might keep them from wholly understanding how costly freedom is, or how meaningful the cost is to those who have been to war in defense of America. Tyler said:

"People don't understand the disassociate behaviors we [veterans] go through and I get angry at civilians, because they get caught up in some pretty dumb meaningless stuff, and they really don't understand what some boys had to do for them. Many civilians really don't understand how America works and they don't appreciate how lucky they really are each day. It's people not taking advantage of the opportunities they have or not taking advantage of our free public education.

What people don't understand is what it has taken to get this country to this point and all this opportunity they are plundering and wasting on the back of the blood of boys like Marc and they don't even care, they have no idea. It's ridiculous.I had a hard time when there were months living in villages, and we would dump millions into training these little militias in Afghanistan, or fixing up a school then I would talk to my wife back home and we were laying off music and art programs at school, teachers, and firemen. I saw this degeneration as an insult to all us boys fighting. In addition to that, I'll fight and die for my taxes to go to people who really need it. There are people out there who deserve the help from welfare, and I'm proud that my taxes go to help them, but those who leech off of it, when they truly don't have to, I find truly insulting and disturbing. That's a problem with America, and too many Americans just don't really understand that."

Part II

In the hunt for information while writing this book, I spoke to numerous military personnel who either knew those I wrote about or were with them when they died. What I was not expecting was to hear the burden from those who shared so freely. I began to see they had their own burden to bare. Originally, I was seeking to share the burden of freedom through the gravity of losing a loved one by telling the stories of what families go through. What I learned through this process is that the burden of freedom is not limited to just the families of those who have given the ultimate sacrifice. The burden of freedom also revealed itself in those who shared their war experiences with me. I first thought this book was going to be about the twelve individuals from the San Jacinto Valley and their families, but this project took on an unexpected addition. Therefore, it is only fitting that some of the stories, from those who shared, be shared as well.

Chapter 15
Cpl. Jim Scherer

I was given Jim Scherer's phone number by Jeromy West's mother while I was seeking information on Jeromy and PTSD. Jim and Jeromy were close friends in the Marine Corps, but they were not in the same places together during the war. As I questioned Jim, I began to see his story developing, and it was very compelling. What follows is the information Jim shared with me, which unfolded in ways I never expected.

I was asking Jim about the effects of PTSD and he said:

"My chest gets tight. I get tightly wound and my anger builds up quick. I have a short fuse," which was something he did not have prior to his war experience. "What caused my PTSD? Some of the shit I saw. Some of the difficult situations we were in."

Born in Las Vegas, Nevada on May 23, 1986, he moved to Wisconsin with his mother when he was six months old. Jim volunteered to join the United States Marine Corps in June of 2004.

"Joining was something I wanted to do since 9/11. I chose the Marines after my dad told me I should strive to be the best I could be."

He was assigned to the 1st Battalion, 5th Marines, and joined them on January 8, 2005. They departed for Iraq on February 28, 2005 and spent the next seven months in Al-Ramadi. His unit's main objective was security patrols and when they received word of a high valued target in an area they would do a night raid with a "Cordon and Knock" procedure. They would cordon off the area and knock on the door of the home that was thought to have the target. The night raids and the cordon and knocks were uneventful.

"Nothing big ever came from the raids. I was never engaged in any firefights. Our big problem were the snipers and the IEDs."

Jim's first fatal war experience took place on Thursday, April 14, 2005, when his unit was on patrol. They were on the roof of a building in Ramadi.

"While we were on the roof we heard the snap of a shot and we all hit the deck. When I looked back about ten feet behind me and a couple feet to my left our Company Commander, Captain Edge, was laying on his back. A sniper's bullet entered about one inch above the rim of his helmet and struck him right in the middle of his forehead. He was killed instantly. We shot back then sent some guys to surround the school where we thought the shot came from, but we never caught the shooter. We got our asses chewed for shooting back and not knowing exactly where the shot came from. We were not allowed to shoot back unless we were one-hundred percent sure we knew where they were shooting from. It was frustrating not being allowed to shoot back, or not knowing where they were, or when they would hit us next."

One of the most dangerous things an infantry man could have done in Iraq, especially in a city like Ramadi or Fallujah, was to be on a rooftop. The worst thing to do on a roof was to stand up where they could be seen for more than about five seconds or poke their head up in the same place more than two or three times. The chances of catching a bullet in the head were highly probable.

According to a fellow Marine that Jim put me in touch with, Cpl. Keith Davis, Captain Edge was worried about snipers the most and it was a sniper that got him. On that day, Captain Edge had two or three different types of radios with antennas coming off of them. He had a visible rank emblem on his body armor and stood up in one place for more than five seconds on a roof that had a parapet about two feet high. The parapet was not high enough to shield him from a sniper's bullet.

Cpl Keith Davis put me in touch with Cpl. Donald Ball who was standing next to Captain Edge. Cpl. Ball said:

> "I was about his 8 O' Clock position when we heard the shot. It hit so quickly and fast I didn't have any comprehension of what just happened, but I knew somebody just shot at us. I dropped to my haunches and in my peripheral vision that's where I was able to see Captain Edge. He just fell backwards. We went over to him and started ripping his clothes off but we couldn't tell where he was hit. Then we took his helmet off and we knew right away what happened."

Captain Edge was a 1996 graduate of Virginia Military Institute in Lexington, Virginia. It was his second tour of Iraq and his first time in command of Bravo Company, 1st Battalion, 5th Marine Regiment. He was assigned to them about four months before they left for Iraq and was thought of by his men as ". . . a really good guy. Extremely confident, brave, and very fair." He left behind his mother, father, two brothers, his wife Krissy, and his two young daughters.

Six weeks later, on May 30, 2005, Jim's friend Cpl Jeffrey B. Starr was on his third to last patrol before going home. Jim said:

> "I wasn't there when it happened. I just heard about it. He was hit by a sniper while on a patrol. A medic was right on him, but he couldn't save him. I was told the sniper's bullet went through the arm hole opening on his body armor and hit him in the chest."

Jim informed me that Cpl. Keith Davis, was present when Cpl. Starr was hit. Cpl. Davis said:

"On this day, we loaded up on the seven-ton transport trucks. I was in the back and Starr was up in the cab with the vehicle commander. When we arrived at the drop-off point for the foot patrol I began to get out of the back of the seven -ton, and I fell on my butt. Starr kind of jumped out of the cab ran over to me and said, 'Are you okay?' I could tell right then and there he was being a little weird that day, because normally he would have laughed at me. So, I got up and dusted myself off then walked over to the side where we were going to assemble into our positions to get ready to do foot patrol. Our squad was in the middle of the platoon, and you got the point position for the squad, you got the middle position you got the tail end, Charlie position. Starr liked to be in the middle, because in the middle if you get attacked in the front, or if you get attacked in the rear, it's the same distance from the attack both ways and when you get attacked in the middle the guys are ready.

The second thing I thought was really weird that day was that when I walked up to Starr I was going to ask him if he wanted to take point for the squad and before I could get any words out he said, 'I got point.' And it registered to me at that time he really was acting different that day.

We started off on patrol and about twenty seconds into it he was crossing an alley way. I remember I looked down at my boots, and I heard the crack then the round impacting and I looked up, and I immediately looked at Starr because I knew that he was the one that would be in danger at that point. When I looked at him, it was like it was in slow motion. I could see the dust flying off of him, like something hard hit him and he was spinning to his right, clockwise. All our junior guys just kind of froze. I ran towards him yelling, 'Corp. Man up, Corp. Man up.' I had about thirty yards to cover. As I was running toward him I remember he spun and then dropped then he started to get back up and fell back down. By that time, I reached him and I knelt down next to him in front of the alley. I reached down. I grabbed him and I saw blood off of his left shoulder.

The bullet went into one of the small openings of his flak-jacket so it was either a very good marksman or an extremely lucky shot. I looked right into his eyes and his bright blue eyes just turned a steel grey as the life just went out of them. Then his eyes rolled to the back of his head. I honestly thought he had just passed out. I was trying to pull him one way out of the alley way, and I couldn't pull him. His body weighed ten times as much and I'm thinking 'Geez why is he so heavy,' and I looked up and I noticed one of our junior Marines, Rivera, was actually trying to pull him in the opposite direction, because he didn't see me. Needless to say, he kind of had the tunnel vision thing going so I let go, and they pulled him in the opposite direction and our Corp. man started to work on him.

One of my buddies saw where the sniper shot came from so I radioed that in and the lieutenant gave me the go ahead to counter attack. We arrived at the shooter's location about one minute later, but the guy was gone. He escaped through a hole in the back wall that led to an alley way. This guy even picked up his brass shells so he was a real professional, but these guys eventually always get caught or killed.

We found out twenty or thirty minutes later that Starr had died. I was the last person Jeffery Starr saw before he died.

I didn't think about it till later, but I think he knew he was going to die. The week before his death he kept saying to me, 'Do you think Captain Edge knew it was coming? Do you think he felt that?' Because Captain Edge was worried about snipers the most and it was a sniper that got him. Because Starr was so intelligent I just kind of brushed him off as an inquisitive mind, not really thinking if maybe he was feeling the same way and wanted to know if it was possible to actually know if you could feel it coming. He was very ambitious, very intelligent, very funny, and just a great and fun guy to be around. He seemed to have everything figured out. If there was anybody who could have gone on to be President or something like that, not the politician type, the complete opposite, he was the one."

War is unpredictable and random at times and the IED is a perfect example of that unpredictable randomness. Jim Scherer said:

"One day we were driving in a truck we called a ten-pax. It had benches in the back that could hold five personnel on each side. I was seated closest to the cab directly behind the passenger in the cab with two guys to my left. There were three guys sitting directly across from us. As we were driving along we were laughing and cracking jokes when it (IED) hit us. The blast came from somewhere underneath the driver, but missed the driver completely. The passenger in the cab, Cpl. Keith Davis, took a piece of shrapnel in the ankle and it knocked him out of commission for a few weeks. The guy sitting directly across from me took some shrapnel in the ass, and it split his left triceps muscle in two. The guy next to him took three pieces of shrapnel in the lower back and he said some hit him in the ass, but I couldn't see any blood coming from his ass area and the guy next to him didn't get a scratch on him. I also didn't get a single scratch on me, but the guy next to me was knocked out cold and the guy next to him took small pieces of shrapnel in the knee."

Cpl. Keith Davis spent three weeks recovering from his ankle wound. The day he was released from the hospital, August 3, 2005, he went back on patrol. Jim said:

"It was his first patrol back from his injury and I heard he just stepped out of his vehicle when a sniper's bullet struck him in the left hip and he ended up losing his left leg."

Cpl. Keith Davis survived his wound and said this about his experience:

"We came out of a house into an alley way that was about twelve- feet wide and it was lined on both sides by twelve- foot high brick walls. The whole length of the alley was about one hundred yards. We probably had about twenty-five to thirty yards left until we cleared the alley once we exited the house. I was the last guy out of the house. I turned to my left and went about ten paces before I turned around to see the owner of the house we just left standing in his doorway in the alley.

We waved a friendly bye to each other and that's when a bullet struck next to his head. This shot hit about eight -inches to the left of this guy's face, and he immediately fell back into his door. I couldn't see where the shot came from, but because of the high walls I knew the shooter had to be able to see us from a higher position. So, I looked over the far wall and there were only three houses that were three stories. I knew he had to be in one of those three. They were about two blocks over and I could tell by the shot he was pretty much perpendicular to the alley. He fired another shot at me that hit about face level and about eight feet to my right so I took two wide steps to my left and kept scanning the windows. He took another shot, same thing, face level, six feet to my right. I took two steps to the left. He fired again. It was four feet out. I took two steps to my left and he fired again and that one was about two or three feet to my right, but when he fired that one I could feel he was getting agitated and each time he would shoot he would get closer to the window he was shooting through.

On his last shot his mussel blast blew the dirt off his windowsill, so I was able to see his position. When I saw the dust, I fired two or three quick shots toward the window, not really aiming, just trying to get him to not fire another shot and that way I could link up with my patrol and we would know where to maneuver to get him. When I turned to my left and started running toward my unit I started getting lit up by a second gunner who was at the far end of the alley. He opened on me with about a forty-round burst from a machine gun. I felt the first bullet go right over the top of my head. The second bullet tickled my left ear lobe. The third bullet tickled my right ear lobe, and the fourth bullet tickled the right side of my neck.

I remember thinking, 'I'm about to get shot.' Then I felt the punch of the fifth bullet hit me from behind in the lower left abdomen underneath the body armor and ricochet down through my left thigh, and then exit the top of my thigh. Everything went numb and I couldn't feel anything. My very next thought was, 'I just got hit.' Since I was running when this happened I was hit right when my left leg was supposed to come forward, but it wouldn't move, so I fell forward onto my stomach.

That was when I thought, 'My third tour and they finally shot me.' My left leg was stuck up in the air like a pair of open scissors and I remember thinking, 'This guy's going to shoot me right up the crotch,' so I tried to bring my left leg down, but I couldn't move it. So then I moved my right leg just a little bit to know that I could move it and know that I wasn't paralyzed. A second or two after moving my right leg, my left leg started coming down by itself in one fluid motion. That's when blood came rushing out of my femoral artery. As my leg came down on its own, Lance Cpl. Jesus Ortega yelled out, 'I think he's dead! then I got on my radio and calmly said,'I'm not dead. I'm fine. Just come back and get me.' My buddies Lance Cpl. Jesus Ortega and Cpl. Clarence T. Spencer ran out into the alley way.

They rolled me over onto my back, and Ortega reached up under my arms and picked me up. Spencer grabbed my leg and that was the first jolt of pain I felt when that broken bone started grinding in the leg when he picked it up. Spencer said, 'Why don't you get up and walk, you're fucking heavy.' I said, 'Because I can't move my leg motherfucker.' So, they got me out of there and these guys (enemy) were still shooting at this time, so I was really glad they came out to get me. And they got me over there and they got me around a wall. They laid me on the ground and Doc. Robinson stripped my trousers off and that's when everybody saw what we were dealing with. Nobody was going to tell me how bad it was so I had to take the clues from around me. The lieutenant who was right behind my head started cussing, then I heard him on the radio calling for medevac and I heard him say, 'Urgent Surgical' which is the worst you can be. One Marine was standing there just saying, 'Oh fuck!' over and over. Cpl. Spencer was holding me and slapping the crap out of me to keep me from going into shock and Doc. Robinson was off to my left doing his thing.

Even with all this going on I knew where the bullet entered and had a pretty good idea where it came out, but I was worried about my nuts. So, I said, 'Doc, do I have my nuts?' He said, 'Yes.' But I wasn't expecting him to tell me the truth, so I said, 'No Doc. seriously, do I have my nuts?' He said, 'They're there.' The third time I said, 'Doc', and before I could ask the question he reached down and squeezed them so I could feel them and I remember thinking, 'Oh thank God!'

After I knew they were okay I just laid my head back and stared up at the sun and let everything take its course from there. One of the first things they taught me when I went in was that this isn't Hollywood. If you're lying there bleeding out don't act like you'll miss your loved ones, don't cry, and all that shit. It's bad enough that your brothers are going to sit there and watch you die, so don't make it worse on them, because that's going to be the moment they remember most about you. How you behaved yourself when you died that's how they're going to remember you for the rest of their lives. That moment right there is going to make or break everything you've done up to that point. I was going to die with my dignity.

I started losing consciousness and I remember Spencer slapping the shit out of me again, but I could barely feel it. It kind of brought me back to and after laying there three to five minutes the medevac guys showed up and put me in the back of the ten-pax Humvee. They couldn't tourniquet my hip so I was going to bleed out on the way to the field hospital. The exit wound was about the size of a one-pound coffee can so Doc. Robinson ended up sticking his entire knee into the exit wound to stop the bleeding, and that didn't feel very good. There was another Corp. man holding Doc Robinson up so he wouldn't fall over and I would bleed out.

So much blood had left me that I was thirsty. I said, 'I'm thirsty. I need some water,' and they gave it to me. Normally they wouldn't do that, so I could tell they were just trying to comfort me in what they thought were my last moments. I drank about two quarts in two minutes, and all my alertness came back. At that point, I put everything together and thought my chances aren't that good. I kept thinking, 'My survival is dependent on one IED. If one IED goes off in the right place I'll bleed to death out here.' What I didn't know is 2nd platoon, who we had actually fought with in Fallujah the year before, had gone out and cleared the route for me, a route that was always loaded with IEDs, route Michigan. They cleared it before the medevac went through. They went out and made sure there were no IEDs out there. I really did appreciate that later on when I found out.

When they got me to the field hospital the medical team jumped in the back with a stretcher to take me out. Doc. Robinson pulled his knee out of the wound, and blood came shooting out. They took me into the hospital and put me on the same exact table they had me on three weeks earlier from my ankle wound. I was planning on making a joke when I got to the hospital, and I was just about to open my mouth and say, 'Hey, I'm back' when my first Seargent ran to me and said, 'You're gonna make it Davis. You're gonna make it.' In my head I was thinking, 'The last possible joke I get before I die and this S.O.B. just ruined it for me.'

They stripped my trousers off. I looked over at the chief Corp. man and he looked over at Doc. Robinson and shook his head no, and Doc. Robinson became teary eyed and he looked down at the ground, then I lost consciousness. I came to five to ten minutes later, maybe, and when I came to I saw the Crew Chief of a CH-26 Sea Knight Helicopter who was strapping me in and after two or three seconds I lost consciousness again and I was out for three weeks.

I did two or three days in Baghdad before they could stabilize me enough to get me to Germany then four to six days in Germany before they could stabilize me enough to get me to the States. I was in a drug induced coma throughout the three weeks. Then I think I was in Bethesda for one week when they tried to bring me out of the induced coma and I remember before my eyes opened I could hear my dad saying, 'Keith, if you can hear me squeeze my hand.' So, I squeezed his hand. When my eyes opened and I saw my dad I thought, 'Now how the fuck did my dad get to Iraq?' I saw my dad for about two seconds. And as far as I knew I went back to sleep, but what I didn't know is that I actually went into cardiac arrest and they had to resuscitate me. My dad said my leg started shaking and my body started convulsing, and he turned around and my mom was just about to come in the doorway so he tackled her in the doorway, because he didn't want her to see it. I was in an induced coma for another week or week and a half before they brought me out again and everything went well.

The bullet took off four inches of my femur, disintegrated my hip, sent bone and bullet fragments into my kidneys and liver, and ruptured my femoral artery. My leg was amputated just below the pelvic bone. It's called a Hip Disarticulation.

It was a well-coordinated ambush. We had three patrols and all three of them got ambushed at pretty much the same time. My Lieutenant said he saw the burst that hit me and said it was about a 40-round burst."

During war, strong bonds can develop between brothers in arms and one of the realities in the life of a warrior is the lack of time to process the loss of a fallen comrade. The grunt must remain focused on the mission first and emotions can be dealt with later. Cpl. Jim Sherer had to remain focused on doing his job while he experienced the loss of his comrades to death and serious injury.

Jim came home in September 2005, and during his seven-month tour his battalion would lose sixteen members to snipers and IEDs. He survived his war experience, but his post-war life would leave him with PTSD. Like other veterans, not talking about it helped him, because discussing it brought back anxiety, which was the case when he shared his experience with me. After three conversations, he chose to stop talking to me in order to forego the anxiety from remembering his experiences, and of course, his choice was respectfully honored.

Chapter 16
Spc. Gilbert Garcia

In my search to gain insight on what life is like for our infantry in Iraq, I was introduced to Gilbert Garcia. Originally, I planned on only using his information as a way to better understand what the lifestyle is like for our military personnel who are housed in the war zone of Iraq. However, as I listened to what he had to say I could not help but notice his own personal burden he carries, and the struggles he has had as a result of his war experience. As a result, I felt it is only fitting that I share his story as well.

Calm, laidback, and very serene, Gilbert Garcia sheepishly signed up for the Army at a nearby recruiting office. It was his senior year in high school and this quiet kid with his composed and relaxed personality decided to follow the advice of his best friend Fernando Gonzalez, who signed up the year before. After a bit of coaxing from Fernando and some advice from a recruiter Gilbert was signed, sealed, and would be delivered to Fort Benning, Georgia for boot camp and AIT (Advanced Individual Training) the summer of 2003, a year after his high school graduation from Rubidoux High in Riverside, California.

Training was completed in November 2003 when orders came. Bosnia would be his destination in December, and with that came a sense of serenity knowing he would not be entering a war zone. But on December 22, the orders abruptly changed and just like that, trickling down from the hierarchy of command, this 19-year-old kid would be going to war. Iraq would be the new destination.

After two weeks of training at Fort Irwin, California, he arrived in Baghdad's Green Zone on April 1, 2004 and was assigned to the Bravo co. 1st 1/60th Infantry which was attached to the 1st Calvary Division. Gilbert's specific job was a machine gunner in a Humvee that was always at the tail end of a convoy. This made him the final line of defense in any procession he was a part of.

One week after arriving, they were given orders to escort two busloads of foreign workers from the airport to the Green zone. On their way back, they were about to pass under a bridge when there was an explosion. Gilbert said:

> "An IED exploded toward the left front of the convoy, but it was too far away to cause any damage. My partner and I turned to look. That's when I heard a strange hissing sound pass over my head, then I saw an object slam against the bridge and explode as the front of the convoy began to pass under it. My partner yelled, 'RPG!' and began firing. I was on a belt fed M249 SAW, and as I was swinging it around to try and figure out what just happened, my partner emptied a 30-round clip with his M-16 at five or six men dressed in black off to our left hiding behind a dirt embankment about fifty yards away. I fired off an 80-round burst and everything was moving in slow motion. The whole battle lasted maybe ten seconds, but it seemed to be moving by like a slow motion dream and once we were under the bridge they (the enemy) could no longer see us, so I was told to cease fire.
>
> I wasn't sure if I hit anybody, but my partner told me that some of them dropped while I was firing. Several minutes after the fight all I could do was just laugh to myself, because I could hardly believe what had just happened.

When we were back at the Green Zone I asked my partner how close the RPG came. He said it passed about four feet over our heads."

At the end of May, Gilbert's convoy was heading down "Route Jackson," a heavily populated highway. Vehicles were not permitted to approach the convoy, but the slower moving procession was causing traffic to build up behind it. Gilbert had to keep holding his hand up telling traffic not to approach as frustrated and impatient Iraqi drivers waved their arms and honked their horns, then Gilbert heard gunfire coming from somewhere around the front of the convoy.

"I turned to look. The convoy was making a gradual right turn along the highway and a couple hundred feet away in the lead vehicle soldiers were firing to their right. They seemed to be firing at a parked car off in the distance. I swung my 50-cal around and began firing in the same direction. After several bursts, all the shooting stopped then I noticed a man standing in a field next to a work truck. I pointed my 50-cal at him and began squeezing the trigger. I let the pressure off when I noticed he had on civilian clothes and waved both his hands out in front of him as if to say, 'I am not armed, please don't shoot,' then he dove behind a diesel truck he was standing by. I swung my weapon around and all the traffic was gone. I couldn't see a car for miles and to this day I have no idea how that much traffic was able to exit the highway so fast."

Four months later, near the end of July, Gilbert was on another convoy run. Suddenly, there was gunfire aimed at the head of the convoy. Instinctively, and with heavy adrenaline, Gilbert swung his 50-cal around.

"Soldiers at the front of the convoy were shooting toward some houses off to the right. I drew a bead on where their bullets were going and began firing. I had tracers and I remember thinking that they looked like red glowing footballs flying through the air. Once we were clear of the houses I ceased fire."

Once they were back on base, he phoned his girlfriend in hopes of finding some comfort.

"After speaking with her for a few moments she informed me that she no longer wanted to be in a relationship with me. We had been together since high school and as far as I knew things were going along just fine."

Later in the day Gilbert would find out that about twenty to twenty-five people were killed in the houses he fired upon.

"The only weapon capable of penetrating the walls was the 50-cal I was on. I think they were probably civilians who were caught in the crossfire.

After being in the stress of war for months and the break-up with my girlfriend I felt like giving up at this point. I was feeling hopeless. After thinking about it for a few weeks I went to my superior officer and told him that I did not want to be in Iraq anymore and I wanted to go home for good."

Understanding and sympathetic to his situation his superior officer gave him a break. Five months into his twelve-month tour Gilbert came home on September 3, 2004 for a two-week hiatus. Born September 10, 1984 in Porterville, California, he moved to Riverside at the age of three with his family and never did he imagine his life would end up being the way it was.

After two weeks he was back in Iraq, and shortly after his return he was exiting a store in the camp when he heard the distinct sound of two mortars being launched from the back of a passing truck just outside the compound.

"Instead of going back into the store I stood in the corner of a pillar and the store's front glass window and waited. I bent my knees a little and gritted my teeth as I waited for the impact. It was too dark to see where they hit, but they were close enough to kick dust up around my feet and rattle the store glass pretty violently."

As his stress level rose, he began to use beer to help him cope with it. He said, "The first time I ever used beer was when I was in Iraq."

Numerous convoys were uneventful, but anticipation made them all stressful. Gilbert said:

> "The stress level at home might rise to a two or three on a bad day. In Iraq, the stress level was more like a seven or eight on a daily basis and would rise to a nine or ten when out on a convoy."

Gilbert participated in numerous convoys that included escorting the Egyptian ambassador, ambassadors of other countries, Geraldo Rivera, Iraqi soldiers and hundreds of government workers, and every job was a stressful roll of the dice with no guarantee that an attack would not take place.

With less than eight weeks left in his tour his convoy was heading south from Baghdad to Al Hillah. Gilbert said:

> "I was standing in my usual place looking off to the right and everything was routine until I heard loud voices saying 'Are you alright? Hey! Are you alright?' The next thing I remember was opening my eyes and I was looking down. I could see that I was on my knees inside the Humvee and there was a lot of dust in the air. I was confused. I looked up and saw the guy in the front passenger seat asking me if I was okay. There was a loud ringing in my ears and I had no idea what was going on. I finally answered him and said, 'Yeah, I'm okay.' I was removed from the vehicle and inspected by the medical personnel and while I was outside I could see that the front end of the vehicle was completely destroyed. The front wheels were blown off and the engine was lying in the street a few feet away. That's when I realized we were hit by an IED."

Other than being knocked unconscious for a spell, Gilbert did not have a scratch on him and nobody else was hurt in the blast.

Being knocked unconscious by the IED would be his last brush with death, and on March 15, 2005, Gilbert was home for good. Hyper-vigilance would no longer dominate his daily routine but readjusting back to civilian life would pose a new set of issues.

"I was having trouble sleeping. Every day I would not be able to sleep until somewhere between 2 and 4 in the morning."

After several days of futile attempts at sleep Gilbert turned to beer. His friends were happy about his safe return. They enjoyed his company until they realized the gentle and tranquil Gilbert had been replaced with a much more aggressive, short-fused, and temperamental being. Even though he was difficult to be around they never shunned him.

"It (anger) just seemed to come out of nowhere. Things would bother me that used to never bother me. If somebody said something to me I was ready to fight them. My friends were also telling me that I changed and I was different."

His drinking continued, and he drifted for a while not knowing what he wanted to do with his life. This uncertainty continued until one night when he left a bar after having a couple of beers with some friends and the California Highway Patrol pulled him over. After the scent of alcohol caught the officer's attention he made Gilbert step out and take a sobriety test, which he passed, but the officer handcuffed him anyway and took him in for the Breathalyzer test. Results showed he was over the legal limit, and he spent the night in jail.

"It was a wakeup call for me. I stopped drinking and started looking for a job. I applied with the United States Post Office and they accepted me."

Gilbert went through all the training and preparation. All he needed was a start date and after several months of honest groundwork and a clean life, Gilbert's day finally came.

He was instructed to show up the next morning to begin his new job. He craved a new direction and a new life, and in less than a day it would begin. However, there was a phone call from his future boss the night before his first day. He explained to Gilbert that due to his previous drunk driving arrest they were not allowed to hire him. A clean record was mandatory for a U.S. Postal position and not even an official diagnosis of Post-Traumatic Stress Disorder would overturn this policy.

"I was disappointed. I felt betrayed. This was the same government I put my life on the line for and I felt like they let me down. They had no problem with me volunteering to put myself in harm's way for the good of the country, but they couldn't find it in themselves to forgive me for a mistake I made. I felt like they were denying me a chance to restart my life in a positive direction, and yes, I know I made a mistake, and I was wrong, but this just didn't seem right to me."

Frustrated, Gilbert remained with his parents and went back to the only thing that seemed to help him cope: beer. It soothed him while under the intense stress of war in Iraq so why not let it console him with the anxiety he encountered upon returning home? Less than a year later, Gilbert met some friends at a bar.

"I remember having three beers then the next thing I remember was waking up in jail. I don't remember leaving or how I ended up there. I was arrested for drunk driving after I crashed my Ford Mustang in a ditch off the side of the road in a place that was in the complete opposite direction from where I lived. I honestly had no idea how it happened."

Since it was his second drunk driving arrest, the courts fined him heavily and sentenced him to community service. Even after being informed that he was an Iraqi war veteran with PTSD, the judge was unyielding for fear that he might hurt or kill an innocent person. Realizing it was serious, Gilbert gave up drinking.

For a while he was enrolled in a technical school in San Bernardino, California in an LVN program, but it wasn't something he felt was exactly right for him. As of 2013, Gilbert still lives at home and continues to battle his PTSD. He sought help through the VA, and he said:

> "The VA has helped me with medications and classes, but the classes were just a group of veterans getting together and talking about their war experiences. All that did was bring my anxiety back. I have found that just not talking about it helps me. I also try to do more calm activities. I have been doing a lot of fishing and golfing lately. They are both very calm and relaxing and it seems to help me stay calm and relaxed.
>
> At this time, I am looking into getting my Bachelor degree and maybe moving on to my Masters. I'm thinking I want to get them in psychology so I can eventually help people who have gone through what I have gone through."

After speaking with Gilbert Garcia and Jim Sherer it was clear to me they both had PTSD. I didn't know much about it, so I did some research on the subject.

According to the *Journal of the American Psychological Association*, January 2011 issue, Volume 66, Number 1, studies suggest that thirteen to twenty-five percent of returning soldiers experience symptoms of PTSD. Some have successfully overcome it while others continue to struggle. This study also suggests that seventy-five to eighty-seven percent of returning war veterans show no symptoms of PTSD implying that personality factors, environmental factors, upbringing, faith, and a plethora of other factors affect individual war veterans differently.

In the past, it was known as Shell Shock, Exhaustion, War Neurosis, War Hysteria, Combat Stress Reaction, or Battle Fatigue. It was not until 1980 that it was given the name Post Traumatic Stress Disorder when it was officially classified as a disorder in the Diagnostic and Statistical Manual of Mental Disorders after thousands of Vietnam veterans were showing symptoms. Never in the history of the U.S. military had the emotional state of the warrior been viewed as an issue needing attention as part of military training. But after veterans began returning home from Iraq and Afghanistan with symptoms, in 2008 the American Psychological Association began to research ways to better prepare troops who are heading for battle and better prepare their families who are left home waiting. They started the Comprehensive Soldier Fitness program, which looks for ways to incorporate emotional training as part of basic training and advanced training. The hope is to prepare the soldiers for the adversity, trauma, and high levels of stress they will be facing in combat.

While researching PTSD I was reminded of a story told to me by a Vietnam veteran named Don Dagne who struggled with PTSD for several years, but eventually overcame it. At the time, I documented what he told me, because I felt it was historically important. Originally, I was not intending to use his story in this book, but after going back and reading what I wrote, I feel it is fitting to include it. Don, like thousands of other Vietnam veterans, carried his own burden during the war and after returning home. Like those returning from Iraq and Afghanistan, it is a fact that life has not been easy for thousands of Vietnam veterans since their return home. What follows is what I wrote after speaking face to face with Don for several hours and after numerous phone calls to clarify any uncertainties.

Chapter 17
Vietnam

As if the physical wounds and invisible wounds weren't enough upon returning home, the American patriot was wounded again by American opinion. A time of peace, a time of love, a time of resisting what one felt was wrong towards the goodness of humanity is what the typical protester might have said, in so many words. Be they kids, lawyers, doctors, drug experimenting hippies, hardcore liberals, peer-pressured comrades, former soldiers, veterans they protested passionately and regularly. With chants of "Bring them home! Bring our brothers home. Now!," and "Hell no, we won't go!" they filled streets across America, attempted to shut down Congress, impeded traffic, publicly burned their draft cards, and assembled, sometimes aggressively, on the verge of riot, and sometimes so angrily to the point of civil unrest.

Donning face protecting helmets and shields, outnumbered riot police would let the protesters know they had gone too far with a crack of a baton across their head, forcefully moving them along, arresting them, and for the most part, temporarily restoring order until the next gathering of marchers assembled for another round of protest, insurrection, and disobedience. It was this type of behavior that served as the catalyst for four students being shot to death on the Kent State College campus when the National Guard opened fire on a group of protesters on May 4, 1970.

With hundreds of thousands of protesters nationwide and their frustrations growing from the war not ending, some began to release their frustrations on the veterans returning home by spitting on them, calling them "baby killers" and calling them names birthed from a hate and anger that came from a place in their psyche that even they couldn't clearly explain. The veteran was re-wounded upon his return home. He faithfully did what his country asked of him, yet he was spat on, degraded and belittled by his fellow countrymen.

"1-2-3 what are we fighting for? Don't ask me, I don't give a damn. The next stop is Vietnam . . ." – lyrics from the song 'I Feel Like I'm Fixin to Die' by Country Joe and the Fish reflected the widespread thinking among protestors. Why is it happening? What is it about? Who are we fighting? What is Communism? Perhaps it was the lack of clarity in the answers to these questions, or perhaps it was the thought of Americans dying in the fight against Communism. Either way, protesters were clear in their statements – "No more war!"

Initially, the enemy was explained as a way of life, a philosophy, and the war was a battle over ideologies, our democracy against their communism. Under Communism, individual human rights are nonexistent. A communist citizen's identity is found in being a part of the whole, and they exist to serve their leaders. Any deviation has dreadful consequences. On the other hand, democracy values and honors the uniqueness of the individual. The individual matters. The government answers to the individual. It is a government for the people, not a people for the government. This was the primary reason for the Vietnam War, the battle of ideologies, and it was not good enough cause for protesters to buy into. Senseless killing in their eyes, therefore, they would strongly resist until America finally withdrew. In the eyes of the protesters, the senseless killing was over.

On January 27, 1973 the "agreement on ending the war and restoring peace in Vietnam" was signed. After America withdrew from Vietnam the North Vietnamese Communists rapidly swept through South Vietnam in 1975. Fear of reprisal from the Communist North forced an exodus of South Vietnamese civilians mixed in with South Vietnamese military personnel. They were hoping to avoid a repeat of the Hue massacre in 1968, when the Communist North murdered thousands of South Vietnamese. Military officers, religious leaders, intellectuals, free thinkers, and anyone who was believed to have helped the south were put to death. It wasn't until the US and the South Vietnamese took back Hue that mass graves were discovered. The South Vietnamese were terrified of a repeat.

As the Viet Cong moved down from the North to capture the whole country, the South Vietnamese began a huge evacuation that became known as the "Convoy of Tears." Hundreds of thousands of citizens and military personnel were hit with artillery, small arms, tanks, planes, and anything else the North had access to. Exact numbers may never be known, but it has been estimated that nearly a half-million people began the exodus and approximately three hundred thousand were never accounted for. It is certain that tens of thousands were put to death at that dark time in world history (women and children included) yet not a single American protester was seen or heard, and for a group so ardently opposed to crimes against humanity, why the silence?

The Vietnam War was about trying to keep these types of governments, politics, and ruthless leaders out of power. However, America's own political uncertainty, perhaps confusion, allowed it to happen. It was a government that listened to the masses of protesters who conceivably lacked a clear understanding of what was really going on in what some called "This God-awful mess," this thing called "The Vietnam War."

Spc. Medic Don Dagne
December 27, 1967

It was a warm and muggy afternoon in Cam Rahn Bay, as Don Dagne (last name pronounced Don-yay) lugged his saxophone toward the lines of soldiers standing before him. The 19-year-old college musician was forced to postpone his college education after being drafted into the Army.

"I was assigned as a saxophone player in the Army's 1st Division Band. Within an hour of arriving, a sergeant told me to stand in a line with other soldiers. I asked one of them if they were in the band. They said they were medics. So, I went back to the sergeant and said, 'I think you made a mistake. I'm supposed to be in the band.' He looked at my orders, ripped them up and said, 'We don't need any more musicians over here. Go with these guys. You'll learn to be a medic.' And just like that my saxophone was replaced with an aide bag and an unloaded M-16."

He was introduced to Joe Bowman, the young medic responsible for training him. Joe was in his early twenties, a 5 foot 9, average build, brown-haired Caucasian, and a Missouri native. Joe glimmered with bliss. His tour of duty was complete. His year in hell was over, for the next morning he would begin his journey back to his wife and two-year-old daughter in America. Don would have to wait a year to experience this same elation. A year of the callous and cruel reality that war has to offer.

Joe methodically explained the paraphernalia in the medic bag and how to use it. A paramedic crash course with the guarantee that he would teach Don everything he needed to know in order to fulfill his duties as a medic. In Don's words, *"Joe was the first friend I made in Vietnam."*

Four hours later, at about 7:00 p.m., Don was on patrol heading down a dirt road with the 1st/20th Light Infantry Division, which was part of the Americal Division. The night was clear, the air humid and muggy. Sticky and sweaty soldiers continued in a routine manner alien to Don. The road had been traveled numerous times, but it was a first for him. Suddenly, on an uphill portion of the road, about three hours into their lengthy trek, a loud sound rocked the team. Foreign to Don, but familiar to the others they all hit the deck. Then the brief silence was broken with shouts for a medic. Slithering on his belly, Don crawled ahead to see what was needed. Two men were down, a well-liked lieutenant who was near the front of the line, and the man directly behind him. The lieutenant stepped on a Bouncing Betty mine buried in the road. Popping up behind him and delivering shrapnel wounds to the back of his head, the lieutenant lay conscious on the ground. After a quick assessment, Don could see he was not hurt too seriously, but the soldier directly behind him fared far worse. The shrapnel hit him in the face, rendering him unrecognizable and unconscious. After further examination Don realized the critically injured soldier was Joe Bowman. Almost instantly, the inexperienced Don intuitively went to work.

"It was as if there was something working through me, because I honestly did not know what to do. I just began doing things instinctually."

He stopped the bleeding, bandaged him, then administered mouth-to-mouth resuscitation for the next two hours until a helicopter lifted him to a field hospital.

The next day, the day Joe was to return home, Don would learn that Joe had succumbed to his wounds during the night. Joe Bowman would still be returning home, just not to embrace his wife and daughter.

Just a few days later, his unit received orders to remove the enemy from atop a hill. Once again foreign to Don, but familiar to the others, the discomfort of clammy, sweaty skin went unnoticed as they slowly and methodically made their climb toward the enemy. They knew the enemy was there. They just weren't sure exactly how close.

Further back on the trail, in the string of infantry, Don approached cautiously. At the head of the line soldiers were very near the crest of the hill. And in the blink of an eye, the silence was shattered. All hell broke loose. Immediately, soldiers at the point began dropping, some from hitting the deck, others from bullets. Cries for a medic rose out of the mire. Springing into action, Don stayed as low as possible as he made his way up the trail toward the shouts for help. Without hesitation, amid the ferocious fighting, he began administering aid to the first soldier he came to. He then had other soldiers carry this casualty toward the back when he was finished, then he went up the hill, closer to the fighting, to aid the next casualty, and the casualties were mounting. Just as he and another medic made it to the last soldier, orders came to pull back. There were not enough infantry to overtake the enemy, and they were too exposed when trying to take them. Instead, a napalm strike was called in. Three jets approached as Don and the other medic tended to the last soldier. Together, they began transporting him down the hill while they kept close to the ground. Simultaneously, all three jets released their first load of napalm. Don and his comrade used their bodies to shield the wounded soldier.

The napalm struck the ridge. Looking up, they realized they were safe to move again. Still keeping low, they began moving down the hill. Their progress was meek at best due to enemy fire still coming from the ridge. The three jets lined up for their second run, this time further down the ridge, on the same side as Don. Once again, the two medics shielded the wounded soldier with their bodies and waited for the impact. They knew it would be close. The napalm struck its target, and Don could feel the heat from the flash. He looked up. The other medic was splattered with napalm gel, *"You're on fire."* Don said calmly. Acting quickly, he used his knife to pop several spots of burning gel from the back of his legs and back. When Don was finished, the other medic calmly said, *"You're on fire too."* He rolled Don on his belly and removed three spots of burning gel from the back of his legs and back. The two then grabbed their wounded soldier and began slithering down the hill again. The three jets lined up for their third and final run.

"On their third run, they were coming right at us and they were going to drop it right on top of us. We tried to hurry, but it was too late, so we shielded the wounded guy with our bodies and just waited. When nothing happened, I looked up and watched them drop the napalm a few hundred yards beyond us. I thanked God then kept moving down the hill. I found out later that the sergeant who called in the airstrike saw the three of us on the hill and radioed that to the pilots and they aborted."

Nine days after arriving, Don was kneeling next to a comrade in a dried-up rice field who had sustained a bullet wound to the leg. Several other wounded soldiers were scattered about as a result of a battle taking place. Don said:

"The last thing I remember was leaning over that wounded soldier then waking up with my face in the dirt and hearing footsteps around me from guys speaking a language I knew was not English. I knew it was the enemy, so I played dead. I could hear wounded soldiers moaning, and the VC would shoot them once in the stomach to give them a painful death.

I just played dead while I waited for them to shoot me. The wounded soldier next to me was groaning and I heard their voices getting close and then I heard a gunshot and the guy groaned louder. They shot him in the stomach. When they got to me they rolled me over and I kept playing dead. They didn't shoot me, but they took my medical bag, ammunition, rifle, pistol, watch, wallet, then kicked me in the mouth until my two front teeth fell out. They had gold caps on them from a football injury I sustained as a kid. I knew if I moved they would kill me, so I just played dead.

It was about ten minutes when I heard their voices gradually fading as they walked away. I waited about twenty minutes before I felt safe enough to pick my head up and look around. They were gone, so I got up and used my T-shirt to bandage the soldier's fresh stomach wound in order to keep his intestines from falling out. Then I used his T-shirt to wrap his original leg wound. I flung him over my shoulder and started running toward the jungle as fast as I could. I had no idea where I was going, I just ran toward the jungle and as I was running, I began to scream and cry, but nothing was coming out, no sound, no tears. After about twenty-five -minutes and running nearly a mile with this guy over my shoulder, I came upon the group of guys I went out there with. It had to be God that led me back to them, because I had no idea where I was going and no idea where they were. Another medic took the wounded guy from me then came back and inspected me. He said, 'You have a bullet wound in your shoulder.' I looked down and saw my uniform covered with blood then I passed out. That's when the medic pulled an AK-47 round out of my back. It wasn't so bad that I had to leave, so I stayed in the jungle with my unit. Fortunately, it was a ricochet that got me."

Within the first ten days he was wounded twice, but he only received one Purple Heart. He didn't receive a Purple Heart from the napalm injury because it was friendly fire.

Several months into his tour he was on another patrol. His unit quietly walked uphill on a trail, each side lined with tall elephant grass. As the procession cautiously navigated the trail, all hell broke loose at the point. They had walked into an ambush. They all hit the deck. Within seconds, the dreaded calls for a medic rose from the chaos.

Don and another medic crawled to the very front where several soldiers lay wounded. Each medic took a different man. Just as Don finished bandaging his first subject, he heard a familiar voice call his name. He recognized it to be the other medic. Don crawled over to him:

"When I reached him, I could see the left side of his face was blown off from the eye socket to the jaw. I don't know how he was able to talk, but, somehow, he was able to speak out of the right corner of his mouth. He said, 'How do I look?' I answered calmly and said, 'You look fine.' He then said, 'Is it bad?' and I said, 'You're going to be fine.

He was hit by an American M-16 the enemy had. Within a few moments shock began to set in and he became delusional. The fighting was still going on, and I was lying on my back in the middle of the trail. I had to keep reaching over my head to grab inside my medical bag and anytime a part of my body rose high enough they would shoot at me. One of the times when I reached, I lifted my knee too high, and felt a stinging sensation just below my kneecap, but I ignored it. I bandaged the guy I was working on then passed him down the line. As I moved toward the three soldiers lying up ahead a sergeant grabbed me and said, 'We have to pull back!' I said, 'But there are still three guys up there.' The Sergeant said, 'I know, but we have to leave them.'

Leaving those guys was the hardest thing I ever had to do in my life. I knew what the enemy would do to them.

On the way down the hill, I kept feeling a sharp pain just below my left knee, but I didn't look at it. When we were in a safe place another medic noticed my knee and said, 'Let me take a look.' I lifted my pant leg, and he said, 'You have a hole below your knee.' A bullet gouged a small trench just below my kneecap. An inch or two deeper would have torn my leg up. I got my second Purple Heart from this injury.

Several weeks had passed before his next incident. He said:

> "We were on a night patrol with no moon, so you couldn't see your hand in front of your face. As we were walking, we were suddenly surrounded by bright flashes with loud explosions. We all hit the deck. They were dropping mortars on us and they came nonstop for about ten to fifteen minutes. When they stopped, I could hear guys calling for a medic. I couldn't see them, so I had to follow the sounds of their voices and use my hands to feel in front of me while I crawled on my belly. I made it to the first guy and used my hands to assess his wounds. I bandaged him up and sent him to the back, then I heard another guy say, 'Hey Doc, help me.' I whispered back, 'Crawl over to me.' He said, 'I can't.' I crawled a little closer and said, 'Grab my arms and I'll pull you over.' He said, 'I can't.' So, I crawled over to him and that's when I realized why he couldn't come to me. Both of his arms and both of his legs had been blown off. (Don broke down in tears at this point while he was speaking to me, then gave me this next bit of information) He kept saying, 'Help me, Doc. Help me.' But what could I do? I couldn't help him. All I could do was bandage him up as best I could and pass him down the line. I never found out if he lived or died."

After six months of jungle patrols, Don was sent to a field hospital at a base camp named Duc Pho. He was relieved to be off of the front lines.

> "I was actually able to get a little R & R there. One day I was lying in my bunk and a sergeant started telling me to get up, but I didn't want to, so he started threatening me. He finally left and I was concerned about his threats. That's when another medic in the next bunk said to me, 'Don't worry man. What can they do? Send you to Nam?"

His name was John Mc Iver, and he was lying in his bunk watching the whole incident unfold. This encounter would be the beginning of a valued friendship.

The two began to hang out together. Their camaraderie would have them share good moments from the past, as well as commiserate, vent, and expel their frustrations about the present. They shared their hopes and plans for their futures. They even made plans to ride in Don's blue VW when they returned home. Don said:

"John saw humor in everything. If a situation grew too heavy, he would lighten it up by finding the comedy in it."

From June through July and into August, the two enjoyed a strong friendship. One evening in August, John Mc Iver sat on a pile of sandbags in the compound. While looking up at the sky, he thought about how bright the stars were and how not one star was blocked that cloudless night. Then word came of a possible attack that evening. How the powers that be knew this was a mystery to John, but they knew. John left the sandbags and found safe cover then he settled in for the evening. Don said:

"I was woken at 2:00 a.m. by loud explosions. I jumped out of bed and went to see what happened. Three Chinese made 140-rockets were fired into our complex. They went through the roof of a hospital ward where wounded soldiers were recovering. When I found the location, I was able to help with the wounded. I found a person that was so mangled I couldn't tell what it was. It didn't even look human. His right leg was severed just below the hip, his face was missing, his right arm was mostly mangled, and blood covered every square inch of his body. If I didn't find a pulse, I would have bypassed him, but instead I pinched off major arteries, dressed the wounds as best I could then had him transported to a helicopter.

There was another guy in the next building over that was lying in his bunk and a piece of shrapnel about the size of a dime passed through two walls and hit him in the back of the head and killed him instantly. He was just lying in his bunk like he was sleeping. When I was done, I went back to bed. The next morning, I went looking for John and I couldn't find him, so I asked someone if they had seen him. That's when they told me he was injured in the attack last night. I said, 'That's impossible, because I was the medic helping the wounded.' But through a quick process of elimination I realized that John was the guy that was so mangled he didn't even look human to me."

The next day Don and some friends took a trip to the hospital John was flown to. Don said:

"When I walked in I could see John lying on a bunk wrapped in gauze like a mummy. As I was approaching him, he rose up, waved to me with his left hand and said, 'Hi Doc!' Then we had a brief conversation. John said, 'Maybe I can sneak off the ward later and we could borrow a Jeep from the motor pool and go get some orange juice.' Then he laid back down and slipped into unconsciousness. This caught the attention of the doctor in charge and she walked over to me and said, 'Who are you?' I said, 'I'm the guy who bandaged him up and he's my good friend.' She said, 'He has been in a coma most of the time. I'm surprised he even recognized you. It's only a matter of time. There is nothing we can do for him. We're just waiting for him to die. He should be gone in the next twenty-four hours.'

The death certificate had already been filled out and they were only waiting for a date and time of death. After that I left the hospital heartbroken. I lost another good friend."

Several months later, Don's tour of duty was nearing its end. In his last week of duty, a convoy he was in came to a stop along an infamous dirt road. Land mines were always a threat in this area and the only way to make it through safe was to have a mine sweeping crew meticulously scan every square inch of the ground. When they were finished, the convoy was given the go ahead. Two MPs in a Jeep led the way. Don said:

"I heard the explosion and started making my way to the wreckage. When I got there the Jeep was flipped over and burning with the two guys trapped underneath. Their right front tire hit a mine the sweeping crew missed. I had to get on my belly and crawl underneath the wreckage to get to the two guys. While I was tending to the driver the gas tank erupted and burning gas spattered the back of my legs. I ignored the burning on my legs and pulled the driver to safety. As I was doing this another guy smothered the fire on my legs. Both guys lived, but I received second and third-degree burns. I was given a third Purple Heart for this."

Don left Vietnam in March of 1969 after fourteen months. He said:

"We were all quiet when our plane lifted off. Nobody said a word. We didn't want to get our hopes up. We were still in a war zone. After a few minutes, there was an announcement over the intercom that said, 'This is your captain speaking, and I just want you to know that we are now completely out of enemy airspace.' That's when we all erupted with cheers, tears, smiles, laughter, pats on the back, handshakes, and hugs. It was finally over."

Don arrived at Los Angeles International Airport fully clad in his Army Dress uniform. "I was excited and relieved to be walking through the terminal at LAX, knowing I would be seeing my family and friends soon. As I made my way down the escalator I noticed two teenage girls staring at me as they rode the opposite escalator. When they were closer to me one of them called me a 'baby killer' then spit on me. I had no idea what I had done. I was shocked and trying to figure out why they did that. Baby killer? It made no sense to me. I was shocked."

Don wanted to establish a sense of normalcy, so he enrolled at Cal State Los Angeles immediately. Don said:

"The war was still in progress, so protestors demonstrated any chance they had. One day my history class was emptied when students heard of a war protest organizing on campus. When they all walked out, I was the only one left. When the professor noticed me, he said, 'Why aren't you going?' I said, 'I have already been there.' Then he said, 'What are you, one of those Communists?' then he left the class. I was furious. I wanted to get back at him, so I studied the material in great detail and made sure to ask him difficult questions every time I was in the class. He started saying, 'I'll have to get back to you on that.' Eventually, he just ignored me every time I raised my hand. I ended up with an A in the class."

As the days turned into weeks and the weeks into months, Don was different now. He was experiencing something he had never experienced before. He had a bad temper. Before the war he was easygoing and laidback. Don said:

"When friends would ask me about the war I would say, 'I don't want to talk about it.'

When they encouraged me to talk about it I would get irate, get close to their face, and nearly start beating on them.

One of the reasons I didn't want to talk about it was because the war was not popular in public view, so I repressed a lot of feelings. One thing I did to cope with my feelings was to focus on college and at one point, I took twenty-eight units and did very well in all the classes."

For three years he struggled with it. He said:

"I didn't talk to my wife about it because I didn't know what it was. I couldn't talk to my mother because I knew she would have a difficult time hearing about everything I went through. I didn't talk to my dad about it because I didn't know where to begin or what to say. I just thought I would have to live with this anger for the rest of my life. But it all changed in my final year of college when I took an English class. After every assignment I turned in, the professor would come up to me and say, 'How are you doing?' And I would answer, 'Fine.' But the more work I turned in, the more questions the professor would ask me. So, one time when he asked me how I was doing I said, 'Why do you want to know?' and he said, 'I can see a great deal of anger in your writing.' I still didn't open up to him. On the last day of class, the professor handed me his card and said, 'If you ever feel like you need someone to talk to give me a call.' So, I took his card and put it in my wallet.

Two months later, I was very irritated and began an argument with my wife. It was nothing she did. I just began to argue with her. In a fit of rage, I jumped in my car and began driving toward Santa Barbara. I had nowhere in particular I was going. I just drove north. Three hours later I pulled over with no idea of what I wanted to do, but I remembered the professor, and his card was still in my wallet. So, I walked to a phone booth and called him. He calmed me down then told me to come back to Los Angeles to meet with him and I said, 'But it will be late when I get there.' And he said, 'That's okay. I'll wait for you.'

He took me to a pinball arcade and paid for every game I played. I was playing aggressive, so I tilted every game. The owner was getting concerned, but the professor said he would cover any damage. After about two hours, I finally settled down and sat with him. I did everything I could not to make eye contact with him. Then he asked, 'How was your Vietnam experience?' and I froze. Then it was like a dam breaking and a flood of tears just came pouring out of my eyes. This was the first time I ever talked about my experience. I told him about my Purple Hearts, the people I saved, and the ones I could not save. I told him about the continual thoughts passing through my head that kept me thinking what I could have done different to save more lives. Was there something else I could have done, or something more I could have learned to save some of the soldiers that died? I told him about feeling guilty for making it home while so many others did not. I felt I should have died with my friends, or with the guys I couldn't save. I told him about my friends Joe Bowman, John Mc Iver, and all the others I knew that didn't make it home.

I talked for hours and my crying slowed to a trickle. Afterward he thanked me for sharing and said, 'I have to teach in a few hours and I need at least a couple hours of sleep, but I would like to speak with you again.' I agreed, and almost immediately it felt as if a huge weight had been lifted off my shoulders. Before he left I told him how I had alienated my parents and hadn't spoken to them in over two months. He encouraged me to speak to them.

I felt my mother and wife wouldn't be able to understand my experience, so I called home and my dad answered. I said, 'Dad, can I come and talk to you? He said, 'Yes.' When we sat down together I said, 'We haven't talked in a long time. And my dad said, 'Yeah, we haven't, and I don't know what we did to make you so angry.' When he said that I just started bawling my eyes out again and said, 'It wasn't you dad, you have done nothing to upset me. It was my war experiences.' And I told him everything. When I was finished, he said, 'We prayed for your safety, but we never prayed for your mind.'"

By taking the initiative and with help from a compassionate professor and a loving family, his healing process began.

His father felt that the more he talked about his experience, the less of a grasp it would have on him, so he set him up to start sharing his experiences at Sunday school. Eventually, all these Sunday school talks transformed into speaking engagements at different church congregations which then led to speaking to kids at schools in their classrooms. Although he could never completely erase the pain of the memories or the guilty feelings, it no longer controlled him, and he was able to cope with his PTSD and begin to head towards a peaceful life. Shortly before graduating college he had to give a speech in a speech class. He said:

"I began to speak, but nothing I planned on saying came out of my mouth. I started talking about my war experiences and the last thing I said was, '. . . and no matter what happens, don't ever send a 'Dear John' letter to a soldier while he is in war. If you feel you have to do this, then wait until they get home and tell them in person. I have seen the effects these letters have on soldiers, and they are devastating. You have to understand that many times the only hope a soldier in battle has is the woman he has waiting for him back home. Without that, they sometimes feel they have nothing to live for, and most of them end up dead within a short period of time after receiving these letters.'

When I finished, the instructor said, 'I have to give you a C for straying off course.' And for some reason I was just fine with that. At the end of the class a woman walked up to me and said, 'Thank you. I was about to send one of those letters to my boyfriend who is over there now, but now I'll wait.' I felt pretty good about that."

One evening, while Don was at home with his wife, the phone rang. Don said:

"I picked it up and said, 'Hello.' And a woman's voice said, 'Is this Don Dagne?' and I hesitantly said, 'Yes.' Then she said, 'Hi, I'm John Mc Iver's mother.' I started to panic. I had no desire to explain to her the horrible circumstances her son died in. All the memories came flooding back, and while I was panicking and trying to figure out how to explain things to her she said, 'Well, I just want you to know that John lived and made it home.' I couldn't believe it."

Chapter 18
Spc. John Mc Iver

That warm August night, after receiving word of an attack, John left the pile of sand bags he was sitting on. He said:

"After word came of a possible attack that night, I headed off to find a safe place. I thought I found one. It was the last bunk on one of our hospital wards closest to a bunker. The next thing I remembered about that night was someone telling me to lie down as I was trying to get up to help, then the ride in the helicopter. I remember looking out the door as it banked leaving the compound and thinking how beautiful it looked as we flew over the base. I had probably seen that view a hundred times before, but somehow it looked different that time. I passed out soon after takeoff.

They began emergency surgery, and I found out later that the blood was leaving my body as fast as they were putting it in. They worked on me for twenty-three hours and I flatlined five times. I was mostly written off as dead, but one doctor refused to give up, even after her colleagues said, 'Give it up, this one's gone.' She said, 'Well let me get it (his heart) going one more time. Maybe this time it will stick.'

I have no memory of those events, but I remember flying up and down the coast just off the shore from where the hospital sat. It was vivid. I was flying with my arms out and my legs stretched out behind me like an airplane. I remember the wind blowing on my face and my body and a comfortable temperature.

I flew up and down the coast for quite a while. At one point, I even flew alongside a seagull. The seagull and I were looking at each other as we flew alongside one another. I must have done this for a few hours before I began to grow tired. At that point, I headed back toward the hospital and flew in through the front door. I remember floating down the hallway and seeing everything that was going on there. I made a right turn into another section and I could see my bunk. I went to the bunk, laid down, and went to sleep."

He did not see his body in the bunk before he laid down, but it was the same bed he woke up in. He was in the 312th Evac hospital in Chu Li, and when his eyes opened, the female doctor, a colonel that had resuscitated him, looked down at him and said, "How do you feel?"

John said, "Okay. Why? Shouldn't I?"
She then asked, "Do you know where you are?"
"Yeah, I'm in the recovery room of the 312th Evac hospital."
"How do you know that?"
John replied, "Evidently I've been wounded, and the 312th is the closest hospital to where I was."
"What makes you think that you're in the recovery room?"
"Well there are only two rooms in the hospital that have blue tile from the floor to the ceiling, the OR (operating room) and the recovery room, and this is definitely not an OR.
By the way, what happened?"

Surprised by his lucid rationale, the doctor told him about the rocket attack, and candidly concluded with, "I am going to have to take off one of your legs." After a couple of minutes of letting that bit of information settle in John said,

"I broke it once and it never was much use to me anyway. But leave the other one alone."

In a serious tone, the doctor replied,

"I'll do everything I can to save the other one."

John said,

"That was disturbing. I didn't want to lose both my legs. I remember joking with the doctor about it then I slipped back into unconsciousness. Later that night, I woke up briefly when Don and a couple of other guys came up to see me. Funny thing was the only person that I knew was there was Don. I remember saying to Don that maybe I could sneak off the ward later and we could borrow a Jeep from the motor pool and go get some orange juice. For some reason, I had an incredible craving for orange juice. Don thought I was crazy, and at that particular time, I guess I was. After that, I passed out and didn't wake up for about three weeks.

When I woke up I saw a nurse and asked her for a cigarette. She seemed very surprised. She said, 'Okay, but I'll have to move your bed away from the oxygen.' She then moved the bed to the nurse's station, placed a pack of cigarettes, an ashtray, and a lighter on a counter and said, 'Go for it, kid.' then disappeared. I pulled out a cigarette and lit it up. As I looked up, I saw a doctor do a sideways slide onto the ward, much like Tom Cruz did in the movie 'Risky Business' with the nurse right on his heels. The doctor looked at me and said, 'You're alive!' It reminded me of, 'It's alive, it's alive' like in the movie 'Frankenstein' with Boris Karloff. I probably didn't look much better than good ol' Frankie either. Then I said, 'Why? Shouldn't I be?' That's when the doctor said, 'Well, we expected you to be gone by now. We were just waiting for a time and date so we could ship your body home.

We talked for a couple of minutes while I smoked my cigarette, then I slipped back into unconsciousness and didn't wake up for another three weeks.

When I finally did wake up I asked the doctor when I would finally get to go home, and he told me that when I was able to stay awake and sleep normal hours for one full week they would send me on to Japan and then to Letterman Army Hospital in San Francisco. My family lived across the Bay in Oakland at that time, and it was something I was really looking forward to."

John finally sustained one week of normal sleeping hours, and he was sent to Japan for several weeks of surgeries. After Japan, he was sent to the eighth floor of Letterman Hospital in San Francisco for a series of orthopedic surgeries. Upon completion, he was sent to the tenth floor of Letterman for a lengthy round of plastic surgeries. It would take nearly two years of surgeries to partially put back together what the rocket disfigured. He said:

> "The blast ripped off my scalp, blew a couple square inches of my skull off, exposing a small portion of my brain. It ripped my face off and pushed it around to the left side of my head while completely blowing off my nose, but miraculously not damaging my eyes. A three-inch chunk of my right triceps was taken off and shrapnel entered my upper left arm severing nerves, which limited the use of my left hand. It tore my abdomen open exposing my entrails. It completely severed my right leg about two inches below my hip joint and shattered my left femur resulting in the loss of about two inches of my left leg."

On the tenth floor of Letterman, he would spend eighteen months in plastic surgery just to replace his nose. John said of his Letterman experience:

> "While at Letterman, I would have to admit that the food was great. The medical care was second to none, and the location was perfect. Under my circumstances, I could not have asked for anything better. It was as good as it could possibly get for someone like me. I was lucky to receive such fine medical attention. I was welcomed there and treated respectfully."

When he was finally allowed to go home, he said:

> "It was like landing on a different planet. This was definitely not the planet Earth I left when I went to Vietnam. While in Vietnam, we heard about all the changes, the hippies and everything else, but it was hard to believe without really seeing it firsthand. We were really not prepared for the way we were treated. Instead of being the conquering heroes, we were treated more like villains. To say we were disappointed would be an understatement. We were actually heartbroken.

To be sent to war, thrust into harm's way on mostly a daily basis, and have thoughts of home be the only hope you have at times, then have people back home treat you with scorn and ridicule is a very difficult reality to ingest.

Vietnam was something you didn't talk about, and it wasn't because nobody wanted to hear war stories, it was more because nobody wanted to support us. Everyone wanted to believe, or were brainwashed into believing, that we were fighting an immoral war. A lot of protesters were just going along with the crowed because they believed all the rhetoric they were fed, and it was the popular thing to do at the time. There were real protesters who really knew what was going on and they were just trying to bring all our troops home before any more were needlessly killed, but that's another story, and it should be told the correct way. The stories that gained all the attention were the violent ones that lambasted all of the troops who were just following orders."

A large portion of the American population was unwelcoming to the Vietnam veterans. In addition to that, the country's infrastructure was difficult for disabled veterans. John found this out through experience. He said:

"The one thing the government (the V.A.) did not prepare us for was how to cope with life after becoming disabled. We went into the Army one way and came out another way with no idea of how to get along in a world totally ill- equipped to have the newly disabled live in it. There were no bathroom stalls equipped to accommodate wheelchairs. There were no dips in the curbs, and there was no handicap parking. Aside from it being difficult mentally, emotionally and physically, it was also difficult environmentally on us.

Another thing I had to learn was how to avoid grease spots, puddles, or anything else that would cause a slip and a fall. That was something I had to learn through trial and error, and there was more error than not. I also had to learn how to use prosthetic devices. Some of us could use them and some of us could not. Since my stump was so short they never could fit me properly. However, they kept trying no matter how much I protested that it fit wrong.

> Due to the uncomfortable fit, I rarely wore my prosthetic leg. I found out later that if I kept using it, I would have caused permanent damage to my stump.
>
> I cannot count how many times I burned food while I was trying to reach for bowls and plates in which to place the hot food on, or how many times I burned myself carrying hot food from the stove to the table.
>
> I had to teach myself how to set up the living room so I could move freely without banging into coffee tables, end tables, chairs, and sofas. I also had to learn how to change a light bulb in a lamp without knocking it over. I had to learn through trial and error, and I knocked the lamp over countless times before I could finally get it right — Ah, life a new, what a thrill."

After two years of being in the States, a friend showed him an aerial photograph of the Evac' Hospital he was flown to after his injury in Chu Li.

> "I was able to tell him exactly what everything was and what each section was used for. Except for the few sections I stayed in while I was there, I had never seen the hospital in its entirety with my physical eyes. I was going off of the knowledge I gained through my flying experience up and down the river. After I explained everything to him, he looked at me and said, 'That's right. How did you know all that?' I said, 'I was there.'"

John and Don were able to fulfill their wish to drive around in Don's VW once they were home. John said:

> "We were at a drive-in theatre when Don went to the concession stand to get some snacks. While he was gone, his wife Pam said, 'Why are you being so quiet?'
>
> After a moment of pondering her question, I said, 'Well, here we are sitting in Don's VW all safe and sound without worrying about mortars dropping in on us or being shot at, all the while we still have friends over there going through that war and all that goes with it.'

What I did not know at that time is that I was suffering from "Survivor's Guilt" and I would not get over it until 1975 when the war officially ended, and the last troops were brought home. The night the war ended was the night I finally had my first good night's sleep since my return home."

Thousands of Vietnam veterans came home with Post Traumatic Stress Disorder after the war. Five years after the war ended it was officially recognized as a problem. John said:

"Today, counseling is available for P.T.S.D. victims, because it is a real dilemma. Whether it is physical, mental, or emotional disabilities, I feel that there should be additional counseling for the newly disabled vets by the older trained disabled vets. What better way to encourage those who need encouragement, except by those who have overcome and are still overcoming. Since I have an A.A., a B.A., and several certificates in counseling, that's a job I would love to do."

The V.A. gave John excellent service. He never had any trouble having his needs met until the '90' when service for the Gulf War vets was a necessity. This problem only intensified when vets from Iraq and Afghanistan needed help.

"The flow of returning wounded vets seems to have overtaxed the V.A. system, and it has made it increasingly difficult to impossible for me to receive the medication I need. As a result of my injuries, I have diabetes. They have told me they can only give me enough blood test strips to test my blood once a week when in reality I have to test my blood at least four or five times a day — once a week can be hazardous to my health.

Medications have also become increasingly hard to receive on time, so I have been forced to resort to buying my prescriptions at Wal-Mart every month. This way I am guaranteed to get them on time.

All in all, war is hell, and pain is a bitch, but we go on no matter what the cost. In war, there is always a price to pay, and every day I am reminded of that!"

Chapter 19
World War II

In 2003, I began to interview WWII veterans who were willing to speak to me. I was toying with the idea of collecting as many of their stories as possible and putting them in a book I was going to title "Untold WWII Stories." One of the veterans that spoke to me was at the invasion of Normandy. He told me about the morning of June 6, 1944. He and a childhood friend happened to end up in the same unit on the same Higgins boat on Utah Beach. He said:

> "When we hit the beach the gate dropped, and we began running. I ran off to the right and my friend ran off to the left. When I was about twenty feet up the beach I heard a loud explosion off to my left. I turned just in time to watch my friend fall to the sand and his head was gone."

We spoke face to face for about twenty minutes when I first met him with the agreement that I would call soon. When I called him a couple days later to set up our next meeting, he had changed his mind and no longer wished to correspond with me. He said, "There are just some things I don't want to remember anymore." At the completion of this conversation, I could see he was deeply troubled by the memories of his war experience, and it was clear to me that the burden of freedom weighed on him. I attempted to sway him by letting him know his experience had historical value, but he would have none of it.

I can't remember his name, but I can still remember where he lived. I also remember by the pictures on his wall that he was good friends with President Ronald Regan. I respectfully granted his wish and eventually lost all contact with him.

I spoke with other WWII veterans. One of them was a Marine named Larry Hale Havens. In 2003, we spoke face to face for about four hours one day and he opened up to me and told me his whole war experience. A week later, when I called him back to set up our next meeting, he informed me that he had changed his mind and didn't want me writing about him. His story was so interesting to me that I pleaded with him about the historical importance of it, but he would not budge. So, I respectfully granted his wish and scrapped the whole idea. After so many rejections I chose to put the idea for "Untold WWII Stories" on the shelf. However, in 2013, I decided I would try one more time to convince Larry to let me use his story, so I went to his home and found out he no longer lived there. After a little more searching, I learned that Larry had passed away in 2010. I was very saddened by this news, but I also knew that I could now use his story. I made the choice to use his story in "True Cost of Liberty: The Burden of Freedom," because after he opened up to me, it became clear that Larry had his own burden to carry after returning home from the WWII Pacific battle grounds. What follows is the piece I put together between the time I spoke with Larry and the time he changed his mind.

World War II was basically the battle between fascism and democracy. Fascism proclaims that a stronger nation has the right to overthrow a weaker nation. Once overthrown, the new leader attains indisputable power over the people, and these people must find their self-identity in serving the leader's desires. They all work together for one cause, in one national community, to fulfill the wishes of their leader.

Under the slogan, "Fukoku Kyōhei" or "Enrich the Country, Strengthen the Army," the Imperial Japanese Army had its' own blitzkrieg through East Asia. Japan's desire to expand its territory and become independent of raw material imports, such as iron, rubber, and oil, justified —only to them— their military storm through Asia and the Pacific. In the process of overthrowing countries for expansion and raw materials, they were guilty of numerous crimes against humanity and replacing those countries' leadership with a fascist Japanese government. It was a government that believed in emperor worship and totalitarianism. The emperor was their god, as well as the head of state and the supreme commander of the army and navy. Therefore, complete and unquestioning loyalty to him was the foundation to the Japanese philosophy. Termed Japanese Nationalism, it encompassed the same basic principles as Hitler's and Mussolini's Fascism.

Pfc. Larry Hale Havens
Northern Mariana Islands (Guam)
July 21, 1944

In the Pacific, American war ships amassed off the coast of Guam to take back the island. Guam was just a small fraction in the grand scheme of WWII. On shore lived an enemy ready to die honorably for their emperor, an emperor who had his populace believing that individuality was an act of selfishness. Individualism was strongly discouraged in Japan, unlike in American democracy. What Japan did not know is how powerful a free nation can become when their individuality is in danger of being taken away. But even fighting for a righteous cause can bear a heavy burden on those who fight it when they get caught up in the ugliness of war.

Spewing geysers of dust, sand, rock, debris, like belching volcanoes along the shore, Guam loomed ominous on the horizon. The pre-assault bombardment softened a well-entrenched enemy and made invasion landings relatively easy in terms of war, except for the far-left flank of Red Beach 1, Chorrito-Cliff, (actually named Chonito Cliff) where the enemy emerged from caves and began their defense. The 3/3 Marine's commander, Lieutenant Colonel Ralph L. Houser, at 0912, reported, ". . . mortar fire and snipers very heavy . . . many casualties." The war was real, real enough to wash away any naïveté born of inexperience, especially to 18-year-old Larry Hale Havens.

With a strong patriotic sense of duty to country, fueled by deep-seeded rage over Pearl Harbor, Larry convinced his parents to let him join the Marine Corp. He was seventeen when he enlisted, and now the untried child would be baptized by fire. Larry said:

"I felt calm as I went down the net into the Higgins boat." He and seven others would motor all the way to shore carrying an anti-tank gun pulled by a truck, or at least that was the plan. Along the way, Larry's baptism began. Numerous bullets whizzed overhead like bees, and bigger shells splashed behind them. "I wasn't too concerned about the big guns; they seemed to be aiming for the bigger boats beyond us, but occasionally we'd get a big splash close by."

Their boat met the coral reef where they could go no further and they would have to wade the last three hundred yards to shore. While unloading their cargo, a second Higgins boat, filled with Marines from the same platoon, came to a halt to their right. As its front gate lowered, the biggest Marine onboard, who was 6'6", stepped up to the opening and said, "All right gentlemen, this is where they separate the men from the boys." And like a period punctuating the end of his sentence, he was shot through the head by a sniper, and splashed dead in the ocean. "That was the first person I had ever seen killed," Larry said. His instinct to want to help his fallen comrade was overpowered by his training.

The training that teaches Marines to remain calm under high-stress situations, a training that does not remove fear, but teaches the Marine to remain focused while in the presence of fear, to control it which can display itself as bravery. He stayed focused on the task at hand: his job, his purpose, his career as a Marine for which he volunteered in order to be part of the whole that would inevitably overcome the enemy.

But wading to the beach would not be quick or easy. In water that ranged from waist high to shoulder high, he walked in front of the left front tire of their truck with his heels together and his toes pointing out. He was told of weapons called "Tea Kettle Mines," nasty little things put in place by the Japanese enemy. Shortly after beginning the tedious jaunt toward shore, Larry saw the lethal power from these weapons. A Higgins boat, one hundred feet or so off to his right, suddenly and violently had a torrent of water blast through the center of it, sending water nearly one hundred feet in the air carrying Marines and their body parts. The boat sank instantly, but Larry remained alert to his job. There was nothing he could do to help.

Heading to shore, he shuffled his feet across the bottom, careful not to lift them, but slide them, for lifting might trigger a mine. Protruding out the top of a Tea Kettle Mine was a piece of lead, about the size of a human finger. Encased in the lead, a glass vile filled with acid. Bending the lead would break the vile. The acid would trigger the mine.

An occasional bump against his boots would warrant a check. Carefully reaching under water his hands would examine the object between his feet, always feeling from the side, careful not to bend the lead finger. Sometimes it was a rock, so he would move it to the side.

If it was a Tea Kettle Mine, he would feel around the sides, locate the handle, which was like the handle of a tea kettle, carefully lift it, move it about ten feet to the side, then come back and continue on. Larry said, "It took about an hour to make it to shore, and I moved about six or seven of them." All the while artillery and bullets were whizzing and splashing near and far.

While on shore digging in was the safest place, which was still not very safe. In addition to the relentless rain of mortars, artillery, and steady bursts of machine gun fire coming at them, the Japanese put five hundred pound airplane bombs in the sand. They were buried tail first with their tips right at ground level, then they were covered with palm leaves and sand. Larry said:

> "I watched an amphibious tractor come to a stop on the beach about a hundred-fifty feet to my right and slightly ahead of me. One of the Marines on board sat on the edge, kicked his legs over, jumped off, and landed right on top of one of those five hundred - pound bombs and I watched him instantly disintegrate. The tractor ended up doing cartwheels down the beach and throwing guys all over the place."

He and his partner would lie in their sandy fighting hole under fire until further orders. Those orders would not come until the next morning, nearly twenty-four hours later. In the meantime, life for him and his fellow Marine was confined to a small sand pit with the surging tide close behind. And moving to and fro with the ebb and flow was a human leg, still dressed in a Marine Corps boot and dungarees.

> "I kept looking back and that leg was giving me the creeps. I was afraid the rising tide would wash it into our hole, so I crawled out and grabbed it by the pant leg and buried it in a hole a Marine dug off to our left. He wasn't there and I didn't think he was coming back, and about twenty minutes later he showed up and started digging his hole deeper, then I heard him yell, 'God damn it! Who the fuck put this fucking thing in my hole?!!!!' then he threw it out in front of his hole."

Laughing under his breath and fearful that the raging Marine might shoot him, he never confessed it was him. All night long the beach was under attack, rendering sleep impossible. A concentrated group of mortar and machine gun fire would march up and down the shore nonstop. The rumble of the concentration would grow in volume as the enemy walked it up the beach, getting closer to his hole, and just a few yards short, it would stop and begin moving in the other direction, fading in volume. This continual enemy fire never quite made it to Larry's location, so being the extreme left flank at Red Beach 1 had that tiny advantage among the few that may have existed at that point in history on that small strip of coast.

The long night dawned. Day two's orders came and at 10 a.m. they headed out to take the hill that lay a hundred or so yards ahead of them. Larry said:

"As we moved out, I looked to my left and that leg was still lying in front of that Marine's hole. It was eerie."

Their orders were to scale the incline and take Chorrito Ridge. The objective originally was to be achieved the previous day, but enemy resistance was too strong. A 5:00 p.m. attack the previous day was repelled by the enemy, thus causing the Marines to affectionately rename Sabanan Adelup (a small hill that lay just below Chorrito Ridge), Bundshu's Ridge in honor of Captain Geary R. Bundshu who was killed in that assault. However, taking the ridge on day two would not be any easier. With effective and deadly resistance the well-entrenched enemy would prove sturdy and stubborn. As Larry and the others began their incline, not a hundred yards were gained when they came under heavy enemy fire. This forced them to dig in on the slope.

Except for the short time it took them to get there, they would be spending their second day of battle in their fighting holes for the rest of that day, and all of that night. The dirt from the hole was strategically placed around the edges of the hole creating a protective barrier. Throughout the night, the enemy rolled grenades down on their position. Larry said:

> "You could hear them rolling through the brush, then blow up against the dirt. We would just repair it each time. They were these little things that were not that powerful. They weren't a big deal."

At dawn, the men left their ditches and made it about a few hundred feet around the right side of the hill before they were pinned down, again. And, like the day before, they dug in, surrounding themselves with small dirt barriers, protecting the edges of their holes from rolling grenades. Larry said:

> "A grenade was thrown into one of the holes, and the guy (Marine) inside threw it back. By the end of the day the heat and the lack of water was more of a problem than the grenades were."

However, the next morning they spotted Marines on Chorrito Ridge who had taken it from behind. Larry, along with all the others from Company A, was freed on the morning of July 24.

Larry survived the Guam campaign unscathed. He did not have a single scratch after about thirty days of fighting on the island. Several months later, in February 1945, he would land with the 3rd Marines on Iwo Jima on February 23, five days after the invasion began. Heavy casualties hastened their arrival, which was originally slated for about a month later as a relief group.

Once again, Larry would survive the next month on Iwo Jima with only a scratch. He said,:

"I got a scratch on my ankle and I'm not sure how I got it, but I know it wasn't battle related."

Psychologically, Larry didn't make it out unscathed. He had PTSD. Back then it was given names like "Exhaustion," "Battle Fatigue," "Shell Shock," "War Neurosis," "War Hysteria," or "Combat Stress Reaction," but it was not taken seriously, and guys who had it didn't talk about it much. Larry didn't say he had PTSD, but it was evident to me when he said:

"About three years after I came home, I was standing at the counter in a hardware store, and when a delivery truck driver out front slammed shut his cargo doors I jumped over the counter, because it sounded exactly like a mortar. It was embarrassing."

He was also reliving a near death experience he had in Guam through a recurring nightmare shortly after returning home. It was subdued for several decades, but it returned after I spoke with him when he was seventy-seven years old. On my phone call to set up a second visit with him, which was a week after the first, he informed me that his nightmare had returned and that he didn't wish to speak with me anymore. I asked him about the nightmare and he told me about it. He said:

"It was at night and I was asleep in my foxhole when I heard a sound. I looked over my right shoulder, and I could see the silhouette of a Jap soldier standing about a foot behind my head. He seemed to have lost his way and ended up on top of us. I looked over to my right, and my partner had fallen asleep. It was his turn to be on watch. There was an M-1 Carbine resting against my left leg, so I quietly removed my mosquito netting.

I grabbed the barrel of the Carbine and pointed it over my left shoulder with the butt on the ground, and I aimed it about where I thought the Jap was. I was about to shoot when I remembered the safety was on. I knew the instant I clicked the safety off the Jap would hear it and shoot, so I quickly thought of a way to push the safety and shoot at the same time. Just as I was getting ready to push the safety my partner woke up and screamed, 'Jaaapp!!!' The Jap swung his rifle and fired one shot. At the same time, I clicked off the safety and began firing. I fired off five rounds, then the gun jammed. I hit the Jap, and he was dead, and my partner had to be helped because the one shot the Jap got off entered the top of his right knee and exited on the outside of his right ankle.

In the morning, the Jap was lying next to our hole and he was hit more than five times. Other Marines told me they heard me shoot off the 15-round clip then start screaming about the damn gun being jammed. It must have been adrenaline or something 'cause I swear I only heard five shots before it jammed.

My partner, George Edward Leroy Hobby Jr, from Raleigh Durham, North Carolina, was hit on the top of his right knee and it exited on the outside of his right ankle, but he lived."

It was this experience that came back to haunt Larry's sleep again after speaking with me. On my first visit with him he shared another story with me that took place in Guam, and I could clearly see he was struggling with guilt from the incident. The incident began on July 26 at 0600 hours, when an estimated fifty to seventy enemy soldiers began an attack from the west bank of the Nidual River's (Matgue River today) high ground on the 3rd Medical Battalion's tent hospital on the beach. After coming under fire and being struck by several mortar shells in a three-hour attack, twenty medical personnel were wounded and two were killed. Larry said:

"They attacked our wounded in the hospital, killed a couple of doctors, and I was mad. I wanted to get even with them."

The next day, July 27, furious with thoughts of revenge the 18-year-old Marine decided he would even the score.

"I found a Quonset hut not too far behind enemy lines in the jungle. I was able to get up close enough to peek inside and I realized they were using it to house wounded Japs. I estimated there to be about one hundred and fifty of them in it. So, I went back to the beach and found two guys with flame throwers and one guy with a machine gun. I led them to the hut and told the guy with the machine gun to go stand at the back door and shoot anybody who comes out, then I told the first guy with the flamethrower to unload his fire into the hut when I open the door, then told the second guy that when the first one runs out, step up and unload your fire into the hut. After the machine gunner was in position I pulled the door open and the first guy stepped up and fired into the building. I could hear a bunch of screaming inside, then I could hear machine gun fire at the back of the building. When the first guy was out of fuel the second guy stepped up and unloaded, there was still a lot of screaming coming from inside, but it stopped. When we were done, the four of us ran back to the beach."

Larry remained in Guam for the entire battle then completed a month of fighting in Iwo Jima. He said:

"We were brought to Iwo Jima early because there were so many casualties. We were supposed to come in much later as a relief group, but the high number of casualties brought us in sooner. I remember getting to the island the day they raised the flag on Suribachi (February 23, 1945), but I didn't hear any hootin 'n hollerin like they said there was.

I did thirty days of fighting on Guam, then another thirty days of fighting on Iwo Jima and that was more than enough. I can't see how those guys in Europe lasted a year. I don't think I could have made it that long. There were many times when I thought I was just going to lose it."

That is why when Larry's commanding officer offered him the chance to make a career out of the Marine Corp., Larry simply said, "No, I've had enough."

When he signed up, his orders said he would be in the Marines for the length of the national emergency plus six months. Larry was honorably discharged on December 14, 1945. He never spoke of the coordinated flamethrower and machine gun attack to anyone for fear of court marshal and being charged for crimes against humanity. In 2003, at age 77, for the first time he opened up to me about the incident. When he finished sharing with me, he said in a tone that appeared more an attempt to explain it to himself in order to attain some relief in the present:

"I've never told anybody about this. You're the first person I've ever mentioned it to. For some reason, it's easy to talk to you.

I shouldn't have done it! It was a bad thing to do, but at the time I was mad! I was angry, and I just wanted to get even with them!"

Like all other military personnel who have seen action, Larry had to make the transition from a trained killer in the military to an ordinary civilian doing the everyday things that lie in stark contrast to the life of war. Gradually, Larry's mind made the change from the hypervigilance of a warring grunt to an everyday citizen with an ordinary routine. What he did not anticipate were the feelings of regret about doing something he felt was very wrong after he had done it. Secretly taking it upon himself to coordinate an attack that killed scores of wounded Japanese soldiers weighed heavy on his conscience.

The 18-year-old's war killing frame of mind had been replaced by the at home peaceful thinking citizen he had become, and the memory of this action was now haunting him. Heavy guilt burdened him continuously.

He was able to go about his daily business, but his recollection of that 18-year-old Marine making that choice on July 27, 1945 kept him from finding his inner peace.

His experience may have been unique in its details, but very common in terms of how he felt, for numerous military personnel came home from WWII with the burden of freedom weighing on them in the form of guilt, regret, remorse, and unrecognized PTSD.

On August 29, 2010 Larry passed away at the age of 84, having never found peace.

S1. Lyle Edgar Umenhoffer

Chapter 20
Seaman, First Class Lyle Edgar Umenhoffer

One of the other WWII veterans I interviewed, who granted permission to use his story, was Lyle Edgar Umenhoffer. Originally, I was not going to include this in the book, but I felt it was important to do so because of his story's place in history and the burden this single incident placed on so many Americans and their families.

"I made a promise while I was floating in the Pacific. I told the Lord that if he ever gets me out of this, I'll serve him the rest of my life. I'll go to church, and I'll do the best I can, which I have."

— Lyle Umenhoffer

The Philippine Sea

It was a gloomy, humid night when a break in the clouds allowed the moonlight to illuminate the ship. Spotting it, Mochitsura Hashimoto, commander of Japanese submarine I-58, began to patiently stock what he perceived to be an Idaho-Class Battleship at 11:35 p.m. Earlier in the day, he purposely ordered his submarine to this area believing it was the intersection for the shipping lanes between Guam, Leyte, Peleliu, and Okinawa. Hashimoto held his fire until the unaware ship closed the gap from about six miles out to just a few hundred feet inside one mile, then at 12:02 a.m. he gave the order, "Stand by – Fire." Six Type 95 torpedoes fanned out with the pernicious hope that at least one would strike the target.

July 30, 1945 – 12:14 a.m.

The muggy South Pacific July weather made sleeping below deck an uninviting and uncomfortable encounter. For the unsuspecting sailors, sleeping top side was much more desirable than the discomfort in the crowded, hot, confined spaces of their racks. Twenty-two-year-old seaman, First Class Lyle Edgar Umenhoffer had just finished his shift at midnight and was lying down for the night.

> "I hadn't been laying down more than ten minutes when I heard the explosions. I was lying on the back aft deck. Most of the guys slept top side, because it was just too hot, muggy, and humid to go below, so I was lying on the starboard (right) side of the ship next to the back aft turret.
>
> After the explosions, I wasn't sure what it was, but a guy near me jumped up and thought maybe it was a magazine or a boiler that had exploded. I agreed with him, but when they started bringing the guys back who were really hurt, burned, and injured we knew it wasn't a magazine or something like that. We knew it was more than that. We just didn't know what.

I went around to the port (left) side of the ship to man my post. I had to go to my station and of course, we had no power so there was no communication. I was on the eight-inch gun turret. As I was standing outside the gun with my buddy Gene Ragsdale, he said, 'I'm going down below deck.' I said, 'Gene, you better stay here until we find out what's going on.' He said, 'No, I'm gonna go down.' He ended up going below and less than three or four minutes later the ship started to go over on the starboard side. When it began to list it went over quick, and that's when I slid across the deck and into the ocean. That was the last I saw of Gene. He ended up going down with the ship."

Two of the six torpedoes struck the right side of the massive *U.S.S. Indianapolis,* about two hundred feet back from the bow, at 12:14 a.m. The cruiser was on it's way to Leyte in the Philippines after leaving Guam. Four days prior, on July 26, they arrived on Tinian Island with a top-secret shipment that ended up being several parts for the Little Boy atomic bomb that was dropped on Hiroshima, Japan eleven days later.

Born on May 27, 1923 in Santa Ana, California, Lyle Umenhoffer volunteered for the Navy because he did not want to be drafted into the Army, and since he spent a good portion of his youth surfing the waves at Huntington Beach, California he felt the Navy was right for him. He attended Alhambra High School for two years then transferred to Mark Keppel High School where he would graduate in 1942. He enlisted on February 20, 1942 and went into active duty on March 23, 1942.

"Everybody top side slid from left to right. I slid right underneath the big turret, the eight-inch guns that were pointing aft. As soon as I was in the water I was completely covered with oil. I didn't have a life jacket, so from the time I slid off the ship to about six in the morning I had to swim and tread water. As soon as it was light enough to see, a guy gave me a 20-mm ammo can to float with, then a short time after that a guy gave me an extra life jacket he had. It was a belt I put on that had two CO_2 cartridges that inflated it. And as soon as the sun came up we could see sharks everywhere. There were hundreds of them.

After I put the vest on, I looked out and saw a group of about twenty-five to thirty guys, so I joined them. We tied our life jackets together and made a circle, then we took the guys who were hurt and burned real bad and put them in the middle of the circle. There were about eight to ten inside our circle and a lot of them passed away. The way we knew they had died is we would take our finger and touch his eyeball and if they didn't blink, we knew they were dead. Then we would take his life jacket off and let him sink in the circle a little bit and once they got out away from the circle the sharks would come up and eat him."

Equally as menacing as the sharks was the absence of fresh water. The urge to drink the saltwater would overpower some men. This toxic consumption would cause the fresh water in their cells to flood out to dilute the brine flowing through their blood stream, causing their body to rapidly dehydrate, bringing on a disorientation and confusion known as delirium. Incoherently, they would swim away.

"Our circle went down in numbers because the second and third day guys were drinking the water, then they would go crazy, swim off and when they would get out ten, fifteen, or twenty feet, you could hear him scream and two or three sharks would take him right away. You could see the water churning and you could see he was gone. I think these were the guys who were drinking the saltwater and you couldn't tell them anything. Their minds were made up. We would tell them don't do it, just stay here, because when we were in the circle, the sharks would just circle around just waiting for something."

Exact numbers will never be known, but it was estimated that about three hundred of the 1,196 men in the crew went down with the ship, and an estimated eight hundred to nine hundred ended up in the ocean. Numerous groups of sailors were strung out over a distance of about ten miles and the group Lyle was in did not see another group until the third day of drifting.

"About the third day, we saw another group out away from us less than one hundred yards and they were hollering over to us, 'Does anyone over there know how to pray?' So, we hollered

'What do you want?' They said, 'We need someone over here that knows how to pray.' So, I said to another guy, 'Do you want to go over there and see what they want?' he said, 'Yeah, okay.' Without even thinking, the two of us took off and swam over to them. When we got there, they said to us, 'The chaplin is dying.' We were all bothered by this. So, the guy I swam over there with he and I together said a prayer and then I said, 'We're just going to have to let him go,' because he had died. They told me he was swimming around all the guys in the group talking to the men, praying for them and giving some their last rites and apparently, he just wore himself out. Afterward, without even thinking, we swam back to our group and we were not bothered by the sharks when many guys would just swim out a little ways and get eaten."

Short naps were the only way possible to get any rest, and very little sleep over four days took its toll. On the fourth day, Lyle was separated from what was left of his group, and he was the sole provider for two other sailors whose life vests were rendered useless after surpassing their 48- hour limit in the ocean.

"I don't remember how I was separated from the group, but somehow I ended up holding two guys afloat, because their life vests only had a 48 -hour limit and if I had let them go they would have been pulled under by the weight of their saturated vests, so I had my arms around each one of their necks letting them float with my air-filled vest."

On August 2, just after 11:00 a.m., a PV- 1 Venture Bomber flown by Lieutenant Wilbur Quinn spotted an oil slick in the ocean. On closer observation, he realized that what he originally thought was an opportunity to drop some depth charges on a Japanese submarine was actually scattered sailors floating on the ocean's surface. He radioed back, "Many men in the water." A PBY Catalina seaplane flown by Lieutenant R. Adrian Marks was sent out to help. After witnessing men being attacked by sharks while he was flying, Lieutenant Marks ignored standing orders not to land on open sea and successfully brought his PBY down.

He immediately began going around and picking up the lone swimmers who were at greater risk of shark attack. Lyle said:

"You could see the guy flying. He made a couple of turns around us, then he brought it in for an open sea landing, which is something you don't do with a plane like that. He landed and started taxing around picking up individuals. He came around once and we waved to him to come get us. He said, 'We'll be back to get you.' He was busy picking other guys up. Then he came around a second time and we waved again and said, 'Come on back!' Finally, on his third pass, he came by and there were these two really big, husky guys that were standing in the opening where they had removed the blisters on the sides of the plane. All I remember is these two guys grabbing me and pulling me up real fast and throwing me in the plane and just like that I was in the plane. I could see the damage that the open sea landing did. There were leaks all inside the plane that they were plugging up.

As they went around picking guys up the fuselage was filled with sailors, so the pilot came to us and said, 'I need you guys to climb up and go out on the wings. We need the room.' So, I climbed up and carefully slid out onto the left wing. I was all the way out on the left tip laying on my belly and holding onto the leading edge of the wing. I was the farthest one out. I was right at the wing tip.

I didn't know it until we were rescued, but when I slid off the ship and underneath the big 8-inch gun turret I hit the screws that come out the top of the hatch and tore up my legs on the way down. They were cut up pretty bad, but I didn't know it until I was pulled out of the water."

The *U.S.S Cecil J. Doyle* (DE-368) had been notified and was on its way. However, it was several hours out and would not reach the area until dusk. In the meantime, Lyle laid at the wing tip safely out of the water. He said:

"They had a desalination device on the PBY and they filled a cup with water and passed it all the way down to me. After I drank the water, we passed the cup back down the line. They filled it up again, passed it back in our direction, and the guy next to me drank it. We did this until everybody had a good fill of water.

They had pulled about fifty-nine of us onboard the PBY and we all got about three or four cups of water.

When the Cecil J. Doyle arrived, it was dark, so they pointed their searchlights on the water then somebody come up with the idea of pointing them up toward the clouds. When they did this the whole ocean lit up and they were able to find guys much easier."

A rescue boat transported survivors from the PBY. Once on the Cecil J. Doyle they cleaned all the oil off the men, gave them fresh clothes and fed them.

"Being covered with oil was actually kind of good, because it protected us from the sun.

After they cleaned us all up they put us down in bunks and while I was in my bunk, I suddenly heard loud explosions, like the ones I heard that sank the Indianapolis. I thought to myself, 'Oh no, not again.' but it turned out to be the captain of the ship ordered that they shoot and sink the PBY that rescued us. The plane was all torn up. Guys punched holes in the wings when they climbed out on them and it was unable to fly, so they had to sink it.

They started giving us soup, then they started giving us sandwiches, but I wasn't too bad off. I don't ever remember getting thirsty or hungry while out floating."

The men were transported to the hospital on Peleliu Island before the Hospital Ship *U.S.S. Tranquility* picked them up and transported them to Guam. They were put in Base 18 hospital, a Quonset hut. Lyle said:

"While we were in the hospital in Guam some guy came through and said, 'They dropped the atom bomb.' I thought, 'What the heck is the atom bomb.' As they explained the atom bomb was delivered to Tinian and they took it over and dropped it on Hiroshima, we figured that we had something to do with it and that we delivered it there."

Along with the *U.S.S. Cecil J. Doyle*, destroyers *U.S.S Helm*, *U.S.S Madison*, and *U.S.S Ralph Talbot* were sent to the area from Ulithi. Along with them came the destroyer escorts *U.S.S Dufilho*, *U.S.S Bassett*, and *U.S.S Ringness*.

From August 2 through August 8, out of the original 1,196 sailors a total of 321 were pulled from the ocean and only 317 of them would live. The sinking of the *U.S.S Indianapolis* would end up going down in history as one of the worst single ship disasters in the history of the U.S. Navy.

The men who were not killed by the initial torpedo strike became victims to hunger, thirst, exposure, and sharks. There were also reports of men killing themselves and killing each other after their saltwater consumption brought them to a state of delirium.

After serving nearly three and a half years on the *Indianapolis*, Lyle Umenhoffer was honorably discharged on November 18, 1945, and for the next forty years he worked for the Southern California Gas Company before finally retiring in 1986.

S1. Lyle Edgar Umenhoffer

Lyle passed away from natural causes on
October 27, 2015 at the age of 92.

MM2. Bill Harrison

Chapter 21
Motor Machinist's Mate, Second Class Bill Harrison

Seven weeks after the sinking of the USS Indianapolis, another sailor, Herbert Ralph "Bill" Harrison, would be making a promise to God; that if he was rescued, he would do all within his power to further the cause of faith in God. Although, it was on a scale much smaller than that of the Indianapolis, it was still a tragedy.

Okinawa
September 16, 1945

Downsized from thrirty-six due to the end of the war the thirty-one man crew was sweeping the waters off the coast of Okinawa in postwar clean up when the typhoon hit. A forty-five-minute delay in putting their desalination device back together made it impossible for them to make it around to the downwind side of the island. As they tried to make the turn around the tip of the island paralleling the sixty-five -foot waves and one hundred and twenty -mile per hour winds created a precarious situation they did not want to test. As a result, Captain Blazer had them ride out the storm in open sea. From six in the morning to midnight the one hundred and thirty-five -foot minesweeper rose up over the six and a half story waves and crashed down the back side of them. A short time before midnight the continuous pounding broke the weld seams on the fuel tank to the engine that powered their electrical and steering system. Unable to effectively steer, the YMS-472 broached, and at midnight she lost her battle with the storm. Bill Harrison said:

> "I was in the wheel house when our cat mascot let out the strangest meow. I went over to the portal to let it in and that's when the ship began to tumble. Everything went pitch black. Guys were screaming as we were being tossed around inside the wheelhouse. It was complete chaos.
>
> After the tumbling stopped I was underwater with a metal toolbox on my chest. I pushed it off and stood up. Fortunately, the water was only about at my waist and I knew I would be able to breathe a little longer."

After abandoning ship, nine men made it to a life raft and were pounded by the storm until day break. They would all get into the raft only to have the one hundred and twenty -miles per hour wind blow them off the top of a wave, scattering them back in the ocean, then they would have to fight their way back to the raft.

After being hurled several times, they finally realized that reaching their arms over the side of the raft and wrapping their hands in the rope-webbed flooring was the only way to stay with the raft. For several hours nine men fanned out around its sides and tumbled down the face of the recurring giant waves, violently chugging along, but not being separated from the raft and their only chance for survival.

At first light, they could see they were immediately surrounded by sharks, and the flare gun, sea rations, and water that were tied to the raft were lost as a result of the beating they received through the storm. Their only support was the raft itself, and the hope that they would be rescued soon.

On the first day no help came, and the men were afraid to move for fear that the sharks would attack the raft, but after a while they realized the sharks just continued to circle them. Bill said:

> "One shark came up and bumped the raft with its nose, but other than that they didn't seem to be a threat, so we relaxed a little."

On day one they found three yellow onions and a piece of wood they used as an ore. They waited to be rescued, but by the end of the day they realized it was not going to happen. Bill said:

> "As the sun came up on the second day we could see the tip of a hill on an island that appeared to be about twenty or thirty miles away. We all began to paddle in that direction, but after several hours it appeared the island was actually moving further away from us so we quit paddling. At this point I began to curse the Navy for not sending out a rescue party for us.
>
> On the third day, none of us had anything to drink and my thirst was pretty bad, but I knew not to drink the saltwater, because it would dry up my blood stream and I would die."

After four days without rescue, two sailors decided they would go for help. They could still see the peak of the hill on that island, so they decided they would try to swim to it.

Bill said:

"We tried to talk them into staying and told them the safest place was on the raft, but their minds were made up. The first boy jumped off and started swimming. He was about ten feet out when the second boy jumped into the water. When the first boy got out about twenty or thirty feet he was struck by a shark. He screamed once, and that was it. Other sharks began to come in and he was gone. The second boy turned around and hurried back to the raft. We were able to get him back on the raft."

No longer able to fight the urge on the fifth day some of the eight remaining sailors began to drink the water. Delirium made one sailor believe he could see the ship right below them. He went down to get some pineapple juice and never returned. Another one jumped off the raft and began screaming for a taxi. After swimming out of sight, he was never seen again.

"On the fifth day, guys began to drop off quick and on the evening of the fifth day there were five of us left in the raft. One of the guys who had been drinking salt water was nowhere to be seen on the morning of the sixth day. We don't know what happened to him. He was just gone."

With no help in sight, Bill surrendered to his circumstances. He felt there was nothing left to do. He said:

"It was about two hours before sunset on the sixth day, and I had made up my mind that I was going to die. I didn't know if I would be next or last, but I knew I was going to die. As I sat there on the raft I looked over at that peak on that island, we could still see it, and as I stared at it I began to remember a Bible verse my mother used to read to me when I was a kid. It said, 'If you have faith the size of a mustard seed, God can remove a mountain'. I began to think about it then I realized that I had not been praying in faith. Up to this point I would pray, then curse the Navy for not sending a rescue for us. That's when I realized that true faith is thanking God for the answer before it arrives and really believing it is going to happen.

I explained it to the other guys and then I told them we needed to pray in faith. Afterward, we began singing songs and celebrating. I had the strong feeling that the button had been pushed for our rescue. After about a forty-five -minute celebration we heard airplanes. There were three Corsairs in a straight line about five to eight miles away flying parallel to us. The first one kept going, the second one kept going, and for some reason, the third one made a left turn and began heading right at us. Here comes the most beautiful plane in the world, it dipped its wing and began circling us."

Of the YMS- 472's 31 sailors, only six survived. The others were victims to the force of the typhoon or the elements on the raft. Bill would move on to be a well-established contractor, raise his family, and become a well-respected man in his community. His wife of sixty-four years, Ida Mae, passed away in 2005, and in 2007 he wrote a book about his experience titled, *Six Days on a Raft*.

"I was very happy to make it home and be with my family again, but losing twenty-six of my shipmates was a difficult ordeal to live through. I felt guilt for the longest time, but the way I coped with it was to talk about it every opportunity I had. Eventually, the guilt lost its' grip on me, but even at age ninety-six I still have moments where it bothers me."

— Bill Harrison

Bill and his friends with State Senator Melissa Melendez

The first chapter begins with,

"I made a promise to God while floating on a raft with nothing to eat or drink for six days, and after watching five of my buddies slip into the ocean. This promise was that if God would send help, and we were rescued, I would do all within my power to further the cause of faith in God and this is why I am writing this book."

Bill speaking to students at Desert Christian High School

Bill kept his promise and at the age of ninety-six he continued to speak to any person, or group that was willing to listen to what he called the miracle of his rescue.

**Author Forrest Haggerty, Bill Harrison, Director Tim Lowry
Oscar viewing dinner 2016**

Bill passed away on August 7, 2018 at the age of ninety-six.

Conclusion

He was born Walter Theodore Hitchcock on July 30, 1944 in Everett, Pennsylvania. He attended LaGrange College from 1962 to 1966, then went on to Ole Miss for his Masters in 1968. He was commissioned as an Officer in the Air Force in 1970 and began active duty in 1971 as an Intelligence Officer. In the summer of 1987, after thirteen years of teaching history at the United States Air Force Academy, he was transferred from his position as Deputy Head of the History Department to a Policy & Issues Analyst on the Secretary of the Air Force Staff Group at the Pentagon. His immediate boss was Colonel Emilio Tavernise, who worked for the Honorable Edward "Pete" Aldridge who was the Secretary of the Air Force.

At the Pentagon, he was part of a small group of five to six officers who handled a multitude of diverse tasks. One included speech writing. Colonel Hitchcock said:

"Since I had served at USAFA, I was tasked to write the Secretary's commencement speech for the USAFA Class of 1988. Although I'd drafted a few other speeches for the secretary, I wanted this one to be memorable. Little did I know that one sentence would resonate as it has! As an American historian, I have always been intrigued with the idea/ideal of liberty and freedom and I wanted the cadets to realize the sacrifices the Americans — past, present, & future — made. So that was the genesis of the phrase! The phrase was then picked up by a number of sources... some to justify the Reagan arms buildup!"

On Wednesday June 1, 1988, in his speech to the graduating class of the United States Air Force Academy, the Secretary of the Air Force, Honorable Edward Aldridge read the speech written by Col. Hitchcock, and in that speech the famous sentence "Freedom Is Not Free" was spoken for the first time.

He had no idea that sentence would carry so much credence with so many Americans at the time of its conception. He said:

"Since then, it has come to have different meanings to different folks!"

Colonel Hitchcock retired in 1993 and is now teaching history at New Mexico Military Institute, one of the top service academies prep programs in the nation. He is quite pleased with his powerful one-sentence contribution to his fellow countrymen. He said:

"I was quite surprised when it appeared on the Korean War Memorial. Since I served in Korea & my wife is Korean. I am most pleased about that!"

To the family members who have lost a loved one, and to our military personnel who have sacrificed and suffered, no truer words have ever been spoken. Freedom has been very expensive to this exclusive group of citizens. Unfortunately, the majority of citizens are so far removed from the reality of what this group deals with on a daily basis that they may never give it much thought. There is a saying on a monument at Fort Campbell, Kentucky that reads:

"Our deaths are not ours, they are yours. They will mean what you make them mean. We leave you our deaths; give them meaning. We were young, we have died; please remember us."

It should be our duty to give their sacrifices meaning. They gave of their minds, bodies, and lives. The least we could do is give them our best effort, as well as never forget them.

No human truly wants to go to war but they do, and the thought of being thrust into the hardships of war is not enough to deter them, because in the mind of the virtuous warrior, 'If they do not stop the iniquity, then who will?'

Volunteering to join the military during a time of war goes well beyond bravery and into the realm of a higher purpose. Only children who are raised with great character are capable of such a feat. They are the strong and the powerful, because only individuals of such quality can put their lives aside for the betterment and well-being of others. Some believe the strong and the powerful are those in high positions, those of high society, those with wealth and fame. But, they are not! The strong and the powerful are the peasants and the commoners who appear from obscure places and unite. They are unknown to the average civilian, yet they arrive, ready, dedicated, perhaps scared, but brave. They volunteer to be thrust into the pits of earthly hell where profound strength is required to exist, and sacrifice is never a hindrance, but an honor worn humbly. Never do they cower. Never do they run. Never do they hide. In the trenches they live, marred, scarred, tested, and tired, and in this state, they protect the free and the foolish, the wise and the weak, the choices we make, and the lives we live. And, there are no others as resilient as they, for they are the strong, they are the powerful, and they are the giants whose shoulders a grateful nation ride upon. Without their sacrifices our freedoms are not. They are the men and women of the United States military. The guardians of our nation.

The true one percent that gives each of us the opportunity to be the individual that God intends us to be, and every day I pray that God blesses them and their families, and continues to bless the United States of America.

Dedication

This book is dedicated to the families of Jason Chappell, Michael Estrella, Kenny Stanton Jr, Charles Sare, Jeromy West, Keith Yoakum, Jason Defrenn, Christopher Webb, Travis Dwight Pfister, Agustin Gutierrez, Bryan Bolander, Aaron Ward, Marc Retmier.

This book is also dedicated to the cities of Hemet and San Jacinto California and to all who have served, all who are serving and all who will serve.

— Your Burden Is Not Forgotten —

www.ingramcontent.com/pod-product-compliance
Lightning Source LLC
Chambersburg PA
CBHW020440110526
44587CB00037B/289